ROUTLEDGE LIBRARY EDITIONS:
LANDMARKS IN THE HISTORY OF
ECONOMIC THOUGHT

Volume 12

MONEY AND THE BALANCE OF PAYMENTS

MONEY AND THE BALANCE OF PAYMENTS

TIBOR SCITOVSKY

Routledge
Taylor & Francis Group
LONDON AND NEW YORK

First published in 1969 by Rand McNally & Company
First published in Great Britain in 1969 by George Allen & Unwin Ltd

This edition first published in 2017
by Routledge
2 Park Square, Milton Park, Abingdon, Oxon OX14 4RN

and by Routledge
711 Third Avenue, New York, NY 10017

Routledge is an imprint of the Taylor & Francis Group, an informa business

British Library Cataloguing in Publication Data
A catalogue record for this book is available from the British Library

ISBN: 978-1-138-21086-8 (Set)
ISBN: 978-1-315-40933-7 (Set) (ebk)
ISBN: 978-1-138-21796-6 (Volume 12) (hbk)
ISBN: 978-1-138-21797-3 (Volume 12) (pbk)
ISBN: 978-1-315-43892-4 (Volume 12) (ebk)

Tibor Scitovsky

MONEY
AND THE
BALANCE OF PAYMENTS

London
UNWIN UNIVERSITY BOOKS

FIRST PUBLISHED IN GREAT BRITAIN IN 1969

Second Impression 1970

ISBN 0 04 332037 6 paper

ISBN 0 04 332036 8 cloth

UNWIN UNIVERSITY BOOKS
George Allen & Unwin Ltd
40, Museum Street, London, WC1

Preface

This book was originally designed to assemble and present as a unified whole the many scattered theories and arguments that together add up to a theory of balance-of-payments adjustment. Much of this theory, however, is a mere extension of the theory of money to the international sphere; and I found myself constantly having to refer to or assume as known parts of the theory of money that were just as hard to find in the literature as the theories of payments adjustment I was summarising. It soon became evident that the theory of money was also in great need of having *its* bits and pieces assembled into an integrated whole. The result is this book, which now consists of two almost equal parts, the first dealing with the theory of money, the second with balance-of-payments adjustment. It is aimed at the student of economics who has a general knowledge of economics and economic institutions but no specialized knowledge of the topics of this book. I pride myself on its shortness, achieved by omitting everything not needed to answer the questions posed.

What, then, are the questions posed? They are, in the first part, what determines the demand and supply of money in relation to total assets, of total assets in relation to the level of income, and how discrepancies between demand and supply affect economic behavior and the level of income. The second part is concerned with the sole question of how market forces and policy restore equilibrium in the balance of payments and how, at the same time, they affect the level of income. Physical and other administrative controls as tools of policy are not dealt with at all, because to treat them exhaustively would require a book many times longer and they are too important to be treated summarily. The main stress throughout is on the operation of market forces, not because I specially favor relying on them, but because to understand them thoroughly is the first prerequisite of sound policy.

Professors Richard D. Caves, William Fellner and Ronald I. McKinnon have read parts of the manuscript and I am grateful for their helpful criticism; Harry G. Johnson has read the entire manuscript and his comments, though not as blunt as usual, were nevertheless most helpful; and I owe the greatest debt to Walter S. Salant, without whose detailed comments and suggestions this would have been a different and less good book.

Tibor Scitovsky

Les Issambres
July 1967

Table of Contents

Part B The Balance of Payments

Part A

Money

Chapter 1

The functions of money

Money is a difficult concept to define, partly because it fulfils not one but three functions, each of them providing a criterion of moneyness, and partly because these criteria are fulfilled to different degrees by different assets. At best, moneyness is a matter of degree, with an arbitrary dividing line between money and non-money; at worst, one might get conflicting orderings of degrees of moneyness, depending on the criterion used. In any case, our first task is to discuss the three functions of money, which are those of a unit of account, a medium of exchange, and a store of value.

A. THE UNIT OF ACCOUNT

The introduction of a unit of account in which to express and compare the values of different goods and services was as important for economic life as the invention of the wheel was for technology. A common unit of account is the *sine qua non* of the emergence of prices—market prices as well as the central planner's shadow prices —and these are essential both for rational economic calculation and choice by the individual, and for transmitting economic information between individuals.

A common unit of account, and prices expressed in such a unit, render comparable goods and services not otherwise comparable; and such comparability is apparently necessary if the individual's choice is to be rational, in the sense of implying a transitive (i.e., non-contradictory) ordering of preferences. There is little information on this subject so far but some experimental evidence indicates that human choice often becomes intransitive in areas where it is not facilitated by a common unit of account.[1] To value things in money terms is man's way of formulating and ordering his preferences; without its help even the consumer's simple decisions can easily become irrational.

A common unit of account, and prices expressed in its terms, also serves to transmit economic information between people and so make possible specialization and division of labor beyond the confines of the family. The prices facing the individual inform him of society's relative demands and availabilities and enable him to behave in best conformity with these. They help him to decide what to specialize on as a seller, in what proportions to buy and combine different things as a buyer. Most people become fully aware of their dependence on money prices as means of communication only at times when these cease, for some reason, to fulfil this function. Witness a novelist's description of the German hyperinflation: "Money was rapidly ebbing away from between men, leaving them desperately incommunicado like men rendered voiceless by an intervening vacuum; millions, still heaped on top of each other in human cities yet forced to live separate, each like some solitary predatory beast."[2]

Producers no less than householders are dependent on money to provide the lines of communication, and on money prices to furnish the information on whose basis to make the production decisions that will maximize profits. When money is absent, or ceases to fulfil its function, it becomes much more difficult and costly to obtain this information. This, too, was well illustrated by the German hyperinflation of 1923. In an environment where money prices and money

[1]Cf. Kenneth O. May, "Intransitivity, Utility, and the Aggregations of Preference Patterns," *Econometrica* Vol. 22 (1954) pp. 1–13.

[2]Cf. Richard Hughes, *The Fox in the Attic,* p. 114 of the Penguin paperback edition.

values had become virtually meaningless, business firms were forced to expand their office staffs in order to deal with the greatly expanded task of obtaining and interpreting market information. The ratio of office ("non-productive") to production workers in the Siemens-Schuckert firm (Germany's equivalent to General Electric) increased by 43 per cent; and much the same happened in other firms.[3]

All this shows the need for money, and for the public to think and be able to think in terms of money, as conditions of efficient economic organization and development. A person must know money prices to decide in which of his possible activities he would be the most useful to society, and the most highly paid by it. He again needs to know prices to determine how best to perform this activity and how best to mix his own labor and know-how with other factors of production, and he needs prices if he is to choose the best form in which to consume his income and enjoy the fruits of his labor.

B. THE MEDIUM OF EXCHANGE

The advantage of having a medium of exchange is that it avoids barter; and the clumsiness, inconvenience, and inefficiency that barter entails. To appreciate therefore the advantages of money as a medium of exchange, one must first become aware of the disadvantages of barter.

In his idealized and oversimplified picture of the economy, the economist often visualizes all market transactions as basically barter. People sell goods and perform services in order to obtain other goods and services in exchange. If so, actual barter best symbolizes the underlying realities of economic life; why then is the use of money preferable? There are three reasons for this.

First, as everyone who has lived with it knows, barter is a much more complex transaction than either buying or selling for money. One need not go to the Trobriand Islands to find this out, every economy reverts to barter in hyperinflationary times. In such times, the flow of food from farms to cities is interrupted; because barter is too complex, too costly, and too risky for middlemen to handle.

[3]Cf. C. Bresciani-Turroni, *The Economics of Inflation* (Allen & Unwin, London, 1931). p. 217.

Housewives must go to the country for their weekly shopping, taking along not only a shopping list but also a well-assorted bundle of goods to pay with, which may have to contain anything from china and bed-linen to a grand piano. The problem is one not only of transportation but also of ingenuity in guessing what farmers and their wives want. Moreover, each housewife must find the particular farmer who (or whose wife) wants the particular consumers' durables she can pay with. In short, the complexity of barter stems from its being both a sale and a purchase and so involving *two* economic decisions: what, how much, and on what terms to sell; and what, how much, and on what terms to buy. Merging these two decisions into one complicates the decision maker's problem by doubling the number of variables that enter into it: thus, given the limitations of man's brain, it diminishes the degree of rationality he can bring to the solution of his problem. Therefore the use of money as a medium of exchange, and the consequent breaking down of every barter transaction into separate sales and purchases, make possible a division of labor in the decision-making process that yields returns in terms of increased rationality. I can deal more effectively with the problem of how best to sell my services while free from the worry over how best to spend the proceeds; at the same time, however, I need to know generally how valuable, in terms of spending power, the proceeds will be. Money is helpful in both respects. The money economy enables one to deal with the separate problems of buying and selling one at a time; the value one attributes to money provides the general background information needed to deal with each. This combination of having one's mind freed from too much detail and yet being provided with background information is worth stressing, because our economic decisions benefit from it, while the economist's analysis of these decisions often does not.[4]

Second, the use of money reduces the number of transactions needed to achieve a given degree of specialization. Although a single barter equals a sale *and* a purchase, trading partners who would be satisfied by a single barter can seldom be found, because only in the

[4]The analysis of spending behavior suffers, for example, from the assumption usually made that the household's income is given and uninfluenced by its spending decisions. There is increasing evidence that hours worked, number of family members working, and hence family income earned also depend on spending habits.

rarest cases would the goods and services one person has to offer match exactly the particular goods and services another person wants to obtain. As a rule, to make possible a mutually satisfactory barter transaction, one party would have to engage in a whole chain of complementary barter transactions and so acquire the collection of goods and services most acceptable to the other party as means of payment. Such chains of complementary barter transactions would often be long and complex, costly in terms of time and effort, and risky unless conditional on the basic transaction being concluded. They can be short-circuited, their risk eliminated, and the total number of transactions greatly reduced, by splitting every barter into the monetary transactions of a sale and a purchase. The use of money therefore saves time and effort by enabling people to sell to one person and buy from another, or to sell in one place and buy in another; and the wider the acceptability of money as a means of payment, the greater is the saving. In short, money makes possible multilateral trade. The same exchange of goods and services could be achieved through the bilateralism of barter; but it would be more clumsy, require many more transactions, and the careful coordination of these transactions.

The time and effort saved by the use of money as a medium of exchange is very substantial. Since hyperinflations are the occasions when money ceases to fulfil this function, their study provides the basis for a quantitative estimate of the worth (welfare gain) to the users of money, both firms and households, of having it as a medium of exchange and so avoiding the clumsiness and complexity of barter. Bailey made estimates of this gain, or "the cost to society of abandoning money entirely," for seven different hyperinflations; and they range from 14 to 48 per cent of the national product.[5] These estimates are very rough and likely to err on the high side, since they show the cost of abandoning money to people accustomed to its use. Habituation to doing without money would probably lower this cost; indeed the lowest estimate, 14 per cent of the national product, relates to the Hungarian hyperinflation of 1946, the second within the lifetime of the same generation. Such an estimate does not mean that the national product would be that much smaller in the absence of a

[5]Cf. M. J. Bailey, "The Welfare Cost of Inflationary Finance," *Journal of Political Economy*, Vol. 64 (1956) pp. 93–110.

medium of exchange, part of the loss would probably take the form of less leisure.

Third, the use of money as a medium of exchange increases the number of similar transactions and so enhances competition and the similarity of terms of contract. If a thousand people want to buy bread in a money economy, they make similar transactions, constitute and belong to the same market, and by sheer numbers create a highly competitive situation on the buying side of that market. In a barter economy, the same thousand people would form dozens of smaller, separate and non-competing groups, according to whether they wished to pay for their bread with wine, shoes, haircuts, or some other commodity, and competition would be reduced accordingly.

This last argument, admittedly, is somewhat overstated, because it is not really true that the market where haircuts are given for bread and that where wine is would be non-competing. They would be linked, directly by the market in which haircuts are given for wine, indirectly by the many markets in which haircuts are given for a third commodity, and this, in turn, is exchanged for wine; and arbitrage through these between wine and haircuts would add competitiveness to both the haircuts-for-bread and the wine-for-bread markets. A well-organized barter economy would develop up to $\frac{n(n-1)}{2}$ markets in n commodities, and part of their business would be arbitrage. However, arbitrage is costly in terms of effort, it could yield only small gains in a barter economy; and to imagine speculators stepping in to seize every opportunity of making a profit is to ignore the costs of speculation and the need to weigh them against the gains to be had. Indirect competition through arbitrage in a barter economy would be a poor substitute for direct competition in a money economy; and it must also be remembered that any improvement, any simplification of the complexities of the barter economy would be tantamount to the introduction of money.

The above advantages of money are the greater the larger the number of people who accept it as a means of payment, and the larger the geographical area in which it is so accepted. Indeed, the extent of the area in which money is accepted as a means of payment and the universality of its acceptance within this area are important features and measures of its liquidity. Ease and readiness of acceptance are another. The seemingly nonsensical promise on Federal Reserve Notes: "Will pay the bearer on demand *X* dollars" makes sense when interpreted to mean that that particular piece of money, being freely convertible into all other pieces of money, should be accepted in payment as widely as they are. Banks hold reserves against their customers' deposits with the same aim: they try to make their checks as widely and universally accepted as is the cash they hold as reserves.

The advantages of having a medium of exchange explain why all societies sooner or later single out a commodity particularly suitable for this purpose and use it as money in addition to its other uses. These other uses are not necessary for the moneyness of money; but they facilitate its gradual adoption as a medium of exchange.

The value of money, its acceptance as a medium of exchange, is a matter of social convention. Each person accepts payment in money only because he expects others to accept it in payment from him. I value money only because I know that others do; and everybody is in this same position. The circularity involved means that to elevate something to the status of money, a social convention must be established; and it is not easy to establish this. One way would be for all members of a group formally to pledge themselves to accept a certain object as a medium of exchange among themselves. This is the way in which the Western World is now trying to establish an international reserve currency; and the difficulties of establishing the necessary social convention through formal agreement are strikingly and painfully apparent.

Another way of establishing such a social convention is for authority to enforce acceptance of a money as payment. This is the basis of legal tender. The courts of every country enforce the acceptance of its national currency in discharge of legal obligations to pay.

A third way is for an important member of the group unilaterally to accept in payment a certain form of money; if he is important enough, and his money convenient enough, other members of the group are likely to follow suit. The use of a currency reserve—one country's currency used as external reserve by other countries—is an example.

A fourth way is for a commodity valuable in consumption and especially suitable as a medium of exchange gradually to acquire the status of money. Once the social convention is established, its use as money can persist quite independently of its value or continued use in consumption. The acceptance of gold, first as national money and still today as international money, is the obvious example.

One more way of establishing the moneyness of something is to guarantee its convertibility into something else whose status as money is already established. This is the historical explanation of paper money, bank deposits, travelers' checks, etc., as so many forms of money.

In every case, the value and usefulness of money, as money, derives solely from the social convention; but to establish the social convention, it helps for the money-to-be to have value for some other reason.

C. THE STORE OF VALUE

While money as a medium of exchange enables a person to buy elsewhere than where he sells, or from someone else than to whom he sells, its store-of-value function enables him to buy later than he sells. Most people want to delay consuming at least part of their earnings; and once consumption is postponed, there are many reasons for also postponing the buying of the goods to be consumed. The greater cost and inconvenience of storing goods instead of money, the deterioration and obsolescence of goods stored, the advantage in an uncertain world of storing general purchasing power instead of specific commodities, the desire to wait and be prepared for later opportunities of making a good buy, are some of the reasons. Money, however, is not the only store of value; most financial assets and some real assets as well serve the same function.

The function of money as a store of value has been the least stressed and least well understood by earlier writers on money. Keynes was the first to realize fully and draw attention to its significance for economic analysis and policy. This consists mainly in the fact that only this function creates a demand for holding money that can be analyzed in terms similar to those used in analyzing the demand for commodities. As a store of value, money has good substitutes in other assets and best fulfils this function held jointly with them. The proportions in which money is held with other assets depend on their differential advantages (such as yield) over money. The demand for holding money therefore is a continuous and elastic function of the yield of other assets; and this fact both provides a demand curve for money and renders its supply a policy tool with which to influence the yield on other assets. By contrast, money cannot share with other goods the unit-of-account and medium-of-exchange functions without serious loss in the efficiency with which these functions are performed. Also, the use of money as a unit of account is virtually independent of its supply; its use as a medium of exchange is not, but a shortage of money for this purpose causes merely inconvenience but not the ordinary market reactions to an excess of demand over supply.

Having enumerated the functions of money, we can say something about the degree of moneyness, or rather about how one might draw the dividing line between money and assets that are not, or not quite, considered money. However, we shall do this mainly out of respect for tradition, because to know where money ends and other assets begin may satisfy a love for classification, but is not essential, nor even particularly helpful for economic analysis. It is needed neither for the practice nor for the understanding of monetary policy; it is not necessary for analyzing the balance of payments or adjustment in the balance of payments.

It is customary to define money and differentiate it from other assets negatively. Unlike bills, bonds, and debentures, money yields no interest; unlike equities, it promises no dividends, capital gains, or insurance against inflation; and it offers none of the services that make real assets (e.g., consumers' or producers' durables) worth holding. If money is held nevertheless, it must be for the sake of advantages other assets lack. Collectively these are called liquidity.

The main aspect of liquidity is the medium-of-exchange function: the ready and immediate acceptance of an asset as a means of payment by as many people and in as large a geographical area as possible. A second aspect is the predictability of the value of an asset at that future and usually unspecified moment of time when it will be used in payment. Shares, whose value fluctuates on the stock exchange, are not liquid in this sense; but predictability, too, is a matter of degree, e.g., the market value of short-term bills varies within quite narrow limits. A third aspect of liquidity is reversibility: a value in payment that is no smaller than it was on receipt. Real assets lack reversibility the most; and for obvious reasons. The extreme example is consumers' durables: a car that loses hundreds of dollars in value the moment it is driven out of the dealer's showroom.

Even financial assets, however, lack reversibility when their purchase and/or sale are subject to a commission or tax, although this may be quite small. Few people worry about the irreversibility of travelers' checks, although they are subject to a 1 per cent or .75 per cent commission.

These three aspects of liquidity are best fulfilled by cash or legal tender, at least within the national frontiers of the country whose currency it is. But if cash is the most perfect money within a nation's economy, why should other and presumably less perfect monies circulate side-by-side with it? The reason is that they possess other advantages which for some people, or for some uses, offset the disadvantage of their less ready or less universal acceptance or their less than perfect reversibility. Personal checks drawn on bank deposits obviously have such advantages; and so do bankers' and travelers' checks.

Most economists will include these in their definition of money, presumably on the ground that the protection they provide against loss and theft is an adequate substitute for a slight loss of liquidity even when this is viewed as the *differentia specifica* that separates money from other assets. If so, they are inconsistent in refusing to accept interest earnings as an equally good substitute for a slight loss of liquidity. Surely, savings accounts in this country and checking accounts in some foreign countries, where they are less used but earn interest, are only slightly less liquid than our checking accounts and perform very similar functions. Yet both of them, and certainly the former, are usually excluded when money is defined.

The public's definition of money hinges on its use as a means of payment. It may be best to accept this definition, but bear in mind that from the economist's point of view there is no hard-and-fast dividing line between money, however defined, and less liquid assets. Degrees of liquidity shade imperceptibly into each other as far as the economist is concerned, whether he is interested in theory or policy, national or international. The truth of this statement should emerge in the course of this book and especially from the discussion of chapters 4 and 5.

This being one of our conclusions, we must broaden our approach accordingly. To analyze the demand for money, we start out in the next chapter with a discussion of the demand for holding assets in general. This is followed in chapters 3 and 4 by a discussion of the pattern of different types of assets, from the point of view both of their suppliers and of the preferences of the people who hold them. This, then, amounts to a supply and demand analysis of money, except that it is better to think of it as an analysis of the creation of and preference for liquidity. The fifth chapter deals with the consequences of changes in supply and demand, first of assets in general, then of assets other than money, and finally of money. The last chapter of the first part, chapter 6, deals with what used to be the main preoccupation of monetary theory: the price level.

Chapter 2

The stock of assets and the demand for holding them

General purchasing power stored up for future spending is a form of wealth. Wealth is a stock of value, which people hold in the form of real or tangible assets and financial assets. An asset is anything of value that is durable, storable, and saleable at a future date, and can thus be used for storing value. Besides serving as a store of value, most assets also provide a yield to the owner. Tangible assets yield a service in consumption or production, most financial assets yield interest, dividends, or capital gains. Money alone among financial assets has no yield—none, that is, in times of stable prices.

A. THE STOCK OF ASSETS

Real or tangible assets consist of producers' and consumers' durable goods of all kinds, land and its improvements including buildings and structures, and inventories of producers' and consumers' non-durables and materials. The stock of real assets therefore is largely the result of the past production and accumulation of goods, less their past consumption and destruction.

Nevertheless, the value of the stock of real assets is not simply the cumulative sum of the value of past net investments. For one thing, land is an asset; for another, the value of an asset reflects not only the cost of the resources invested but also the success or failure, and the expected success or failure of this investment. An especially successful investment, successful because it has created capacity that caters to an especially urgent demand or exploits an especially favorable market situation, will yield an income far in excess of the market rate of interest on the funds invested. Its value as an asset therefore, obtained by capitalizing this income at the market rate of interest, will exceed in like proportion the cost that has gone into building it. In general, any change in conditions subsequent to the creation of an asset can lead to windfall gains or losses that disrupt the initial relation between the value of an asset and its initial cost of production.

With the notable exception of real estate, real assets are not a very good store of value. Producers' and consumers' durable goods depreciate at a fast rate, owing partly to the rapidity of technical progress, partly to deliberately built-in obsolescence; inventories of materials and products create storage problems and storage costs; most producers' equipment is too specialized to have a good second-hand market; and there is a hard-and-fast separation of the new and second-hand markets in most durable goods. Most real assets, therefore, are held primarily for the services they yield in production or consumption, and their store-of-value function is regarded as a by-product.

In the modern economy, a large part of this by-product is separated from the primary function of real assets by the issue of financial assets against the security of the real assets. This enables a person who wants to hold real assets primarily for their services to borrow most of the capital (purchasing power) immobilized in his real assets; whereas the person he borrows from, the buyer of the financial assets, obtains a store of value without the services (and the possible nuisance value) of the real assets. In general, he who wants to hold in storage less purchasing power than his real assets represent will issue debt (financial assets) against some of his real assets; he who wants to hold more will hold financial assets in addition to his real assets; and people who want to change the nature (e.g., liquidity or yield characteristics) of their stock of wealth will go into debt and hold financial assets at the same time. Besides separating the store-of-value function of real assets from their other functions, financial assets may be issued also for other purposes; e.g., to separate the functions of ownership and management, or to render divisible the ownership of assets not physically divisible.

Sometimes, real assets are held primarily as stores of value; and in such cases it is often not possible to separate and transfer to others the services they yield. Hence the ownership and display of paintings by the inartistic and, in inflationary countries, the inordinately lavish houses, apartments and automobiles indulged in by people who own them partly as an inflation hedge.

Financial assets are either certificates of a share in ownership (equities) or promises to pay (debts). Privately issued financial assets add nothing to society's stock of wealth and merely change the form in which this is held, since every financial asset issued creates liabilities of equal value. This is true, in the economist's if not in the lawyer's sense, of certificates of ownership, which give legal title to other assets; and it is true of promises to pay, which are issued against the collateral either of tangible assets or of other financial assets backed in their turn by real assets.

Assets can be held by both persons and firms. To every asset held by a firm, however, there correspond other assets (financial assets) issued by this firm and held (directly or through the intermediary of another firm) by persons. When securities' markets appraise correctly the net worth of firms, the assets issued by them (equities and bonds) equal in value the net value of the assets they hold. In this case therefore, the net value of all private assets (real *and* financial) held by persons equals the value of all privately owned *real* assets, whether held by persons or firms.[1]

In addition to privately issued financial assets, there are also public financial assets: promises to pay or debt issued by Government. In contrast to private financial assets, public financial assets are backed not by real assets but by the State's power to tax, or, in the case of cash, by the State's guaranty of their acceptance in the legal discharge of debt.[2]

[1]This equality holds true only approximately. For some personal loans are made, not against the collateral of the borrower's real assets, but merely against his earning power (secured perhaps by a life insurance policy). This tends to make the net value of private assets held by persons *exceed* the value of all privately owned real assets.

[2]Publicly-owned real assets are *not* the backing of the public debt, and their

The creation of the national debt therefore, and of fiduciary money, does add to the stock of assets available to the public. Accordingly, in a closed economy, and when the stock market puts correct valuation on corporate assets, the value of all assets held by individuals and firms equals the sum of the net value of real assets in private ownership plus the value of the national debt and fiduciary money outstanding.[3]

In an open economy, one must add to this total the value of foreign assets and subtract the value of foreign liabilities (i.e., domestic assets held abroad). An important item among the foreign assets added is the monetary gold stock, which deserves special mention also in view of its intermediate position between real and financial assets. Gold is not a proper real asset, since its value can no longer be explained by the demand for its services in consumption or production. It is best looked upon as a financial claim on the outside world, although, since the outside world's promise to pay is revocable at any time and not legally binding, gold is not a proper financial asset either.

It should be apparent from the foregoing that by the value of the stock of assets we mean the net value of the wealth holdings of the individual members of the community. This is the sum of the value of all assets, real and financial, less the sum of all liabilities. This is also known as net private wealth. It is a subjective concept, since it reflects the value that the community attributes to its accumulation of general purchasing power; and, in view especially of its inclusion of the national debt, it bears only a tenuous relation to the objective, or seemingly objective, concept of a stock of accumulated real capital.[4] It is the subjective concept, however, that is relevant for our purposes, considering that we are mainly concerned with the relation of the stock of assets to the demand for holding them and with the effect on individual behavior of divergences between the two.

value need bear no particular relation to the volume of the public debt. Similarly, national currency often is backed by other assets held by the issuing authority; but it need not be and sometimes is not so backed. Part or all of the national currency can be "fiduciary issue", backed merely by the legal enforcement of its acceptance as money.

[3]Minus the debt persons and firms owe the Government.

[4]We adhere to the convention, admittedly arbitrary, of regarding Government debt as an asset of its holder but not as a liability of the citizens or taxpayers.

B. THE DEMAND FOR HOLDING ASSETS

Very little is known about the individual's demand for holding assets and most of it stems from introspection. Theoretical speculation on people's motives for holding assets is largely a byproduct of work on consumer behavior. Empirical information is almost non-existent, since it is difficult to obtain data on this subject from questionnaire surveys, and what little has been obtained is incomplete, inconclusive, and believed unreliable. This section therefore must needs be very tentative. It seems natural to deal separately with the very different motives for holding assets of two groups of people: those who live primarily by their labor and wits, and those who live on the earnings and management of their capital. The first group comprises wage and salary earners and the free professions; the second consists of the rentier, the independent farmer, small and big businessmen, and the corporation. Needless to add, many people have a foot in each camp; but it will not be necessary to deal with them separately.

People in the first group have a standard of living that depends mainly on the income they earn for services rendered. For a rise in their income they rely partly on additional training and the accumulation of skill, experience, and seniority; partly on sharing through wage or salary increases in the general rise of society's productivity and standard of living. They accumulate assets in order to have them available for spending later; and they do this, because the time shape of the desired flow of their expenditures differs from the time shape of their expected flow of receipts. They need an accumulation of assets in order to even out temporary fluctuations in their income, bridge unexpected interruptions in its flow, finance occasional peaks in spending, continue their customary standard of consumption beyond their active earning span into the years of retirement, and leave something to their children.

The demand to hold assets for these purposes is presumably not unlimited. Each person has a more or less definite notion of the amount of assets appropriate to his income, age, size of family, health (i.e., life expectancy and earning-span expectancy), etc.; and the rate at which he adds to or draws down his accumulated assets is bound to depend on the relation of his actual net worth to what he regards as the proper volume of assets he ought to have. In its simplest form, this notion goes back to Haberler and Pigou, who surmised that the propensity to consume out of a given real income must be an increasing (and the propensity to accumulate further assets a decreasing) function of the individual's net worth.[5] This proposition is known as the Pigou or real-balance effect.

To go beyond the mere assertion of this proposition and to try to estimate its quantitative importance requires empirical work, which so far has not been very enlightening, owing, largely, to the inadequacy of the data. Often liquid assets are used as the explanatory variable instead of net worth, usually because data on the latter are not available but sometimes by preference, although it seems hard to justify in this context the use of one in the place of all assets when all can easily be converted into money at market values.

Since much of the empirical work has taken the form of testing Modigliani's life-cycle hypothesis; and since this contains an exceptionally elegant and satisfying formulation of the wage and salary earner's demand for holding assets, we shall summarize here Modigliani's work.[6]

Modigliani's life-cycle hypothesis is primarily a theory of the consumption function. He assumes that the individual's utility is a homogeneous function of consumption at different times, so that a change in his income prompts equiproportional changes in consumption at all points of time; he also assumes that the individual neither expects to receive nor wishes to leave inheritance and saves primarily for his old age. These assumptions imply that the individual's consumption in any year is proportional to the present value of all his present and future resources and a homogeneous linear function of his current earned (i.e., non-property) income, expected future annual earned income, and the value of his accumulated assets.

[5]Cf. G. Haberler: *Prosperity and Depression* (3rd ed. U. N., New York, 1952) pp. 403 and 498–99; A. C. Pigou, "Economic Progress in a Stable Environment" *Economics*. N. S. Vol. XIV (1947).

[6]Cf. A. Ando & F. Modigliani, "The Life Cycle Hypothesis of Saving: Aggregate Implications and Tests," *American Economic Review*, Vol. 53 (1963) pp. 55–84; "The Life Cycle Hypothesis of Saving: A Correction," *American Economic Review* Vol. 54 (1964) pp. 111–13; F. Modigliani & R. Brumberg, "Utility Analysis and Aggregate Consumption Functions, An Attempt at Integration," mimeographed, unpublished; F. Modigliani & A. Ando, "The 'Permanent Income' and the 'Life Cycle' Hypothesis of Saving Behavior: Comparison and Tests," in *Proceedings of the Conference on Consumption and Saving*, Vol. 2 Philadelphia 1960.

Assuming further the constancy over time of the population's age distribution, income and wealth distribution by age, and the average person's consumption function for each age, Modigliani can aggregate these individual consumption functions into an aggregate consumption function of the same form:

$$(1) \qquad C_t = a_1 L_t + a_2 L_t^e + a_3 A_{t-1},$$

where C_t is aggregate consumption in period t, L_t current earned income, L_t^e expected future annual earned income, and A_{t-1} the value of assets at the beginning of the period.

When dealing with long-term problems in a situation of steady growth, Modigliani also assumes that expected future earned income is proportional to and not very different from current earned income and so obtains the simplified consumption function:

$$(2) \quad C_t = \alpha L_t + a_3 A_{t-1}, \qquad \text{where } \alpha = a_1 + b a_2, \text{ and } b \approx 1.$$

Defining total income as:

$$Y_t = L_t + r A_{t-1}, \qquad \text{where } r \text{ is the average rate of return,}$$

saving can be expressed (after adding and subtracting $\alpha r A_{t-1}$) as:

$$S_t = Y_t - C_t = (1 - \alpha) Y_t + (\alpha r - a_3) A_{t-1}.$$

Dividing through by A_{t-1}, the left-hand side shows, in a situation of steady growth, the annual rate of steady growth, n;[7] and, rearranging terms, Modigliani obtains the equilibrium ratio of assets to income:

$$(3) \qquad \frac{A_{t-1}}{Y_t} = \frac{1 - \alpha}{n + a_3 - \alpha r}.$$

The actual asset-to-income ratio, when different from the equilibrium ratio, will approach the latter. The equilibrium asset-to-income ratio multiplied by the rate of accumulation and growth gives the equilibrium savings ratio:

$$\frac{S_t}{Y_t} = \frac{A_{t-1}}{Y_t} \frac{S_t}{A_{t-1}}.$$

How can one reconcile Modigliani's basic assumption about the wage and salary earner's saving behavior with this result, according

[7]Because in a situation of steady growth, income, consumption, and the stock of assets all grow at the same rate, n.

to which the proportion of income saved is an increasing function of the rate of steady growth? Since each person is assumed to dissave in his old age as much as he saved in his youth, aggregate consumption would equal aggregate income in a stationary economy and net saving would be nil. In a growing economy, however, aggregate saving becomes positive. Population growth causes the earning and saving generations to be larger than the retired and dissaving generations; the secular growth of per-capita income causes savers to make provision for a higher standard of living than that which the retired dissavers are trying to maintain; and both factors tend to cause the economy's total saving to exceed total dissaving even if each person spends all he earns during his lifetime. The ratio of income saved becomes an increasing function of the economy's rate of growth and is, in the long run, independent of the level of income. The ratio of assets to income on the other hand becomes a diminishing function of the rate of growth—an obvious result when one remembers that the largest asset holders are the aged at the point of retirement.

Fitting his consumption function to 1929–59 data for the United States, Modigliani obtained the following values for the marginal propensity to consume out of earned income and out of assets:

$$\alpha = .7 \text{ and } a_3 = .07.$$

Assuming an average return on assets of $r = .04$, the above value of a_3 implies a spending propensity out of assets more than 50 per cent higher than their yield; or, put differently, a marginal propensity to consume out of property income more than double the marginal propensity to consume out of earned income (1.7 as against .7). These coefficients also imply, for a 3 per cent annual growth rate, an equilibrium assets-to-income ratio of 4.3 and an equilibrium savings ratio of .13.

Other studies relating consumption to income and wealth have yielded similar results. L. R. Klein found that the marginal propensity to consume out of liquid (not total) assets was about .23, with the coefficient higher for households whose incomes had fallen and lower for those whose incomes had risen.[8] If liquid assets are a good proxy for total assets and constitute between a third and a quarter of these,

[8]Cf. L. R. Klein, "Estimating Patterns of Savings Behavior from Sample Survey Data," *Econometrica*, Vol. 19 (1951) pp. 438–54.

then Klein's coefficient, when properly adjusted (it needs to be reduced to between a third and a quarter), comes very close to Modigliani's. In another study, William Hamburger related consumption to personal wealth, defined as the sum of total assets and the discounted value of total labor income. By using current labor income and property income as proxies for the unmeasurable personal wealth, he derives a coefficient of consumption out of total personal wealth (and therefore also out of assets) of .096. His model also yields an estimate of 7½ per cent as the implicit rate of return on assets; combining this with the above coefficient, one obtains a marginal propensity to consume out of asset income of about 1.3. These results again are close to Modigliani's.[9]

The coefficients and ratios Modigliani derived from U.S. data may also be compared to those he obtained from a synthetic model composed entirely of people who behave as he imagines them to behave.[10] This comparison shows the empirically derived values of a_3 to be smaller and of the equilibrium assets-to-income and savings-to-income ratios to be higher than those Modigliani obtained from his synthetic model. He is probably right when he explains the discrepancy by the unrealistic nature of his assumption that people consume all their savings and leave no bequests. This leads us to the consideration of the second group of people.

Capitalists, who derive their main income from the earnings or management of their assets, have a demand for holding assets very different from that of people in the first group. To begin with, they hold assets mainly for their yield and draw income mainly from such yield. Their income-to-assets ratio therefore is roughly equal to the yield on their assets and generally lower than the income-to-assets ratio of people who obtain their main income from other sources and

9Cf. W. Hamburger, "The Relation of Consumption to Wealth and the Wage Rate." *Econometrica*, Vol. 23 (1955) pp. 1–17.

10This model assumes an economy with rates of growth and a rate of return on capital equal to those in the U. S. economy but populated by people all of whom earn the same (or rather the same steadily rising) income for 40 years, live another 10 years on their savings, and want to maintain the same standard of consumption for the whole 50 years. The coefficients and equilibrium ratios derived from this model are:

$$\alpha = .7,\ a_3 = .12,\ \frac{A_{t-1}}{Y_t} = 2.5,\ \frac{S_t}{Y_t} = .075.$$

hold assets primarily for spending later. Secondly, when they accumulate assets, their income rises more or less in proportion, which renders them immune to the Pigou effect.[11] Thirdly, since their livelihood depends on their asset holdings, they usually expect their children to be in a similar position and want to bequeath to them assets of comparable magnitude. Lastly, to raise their (or their childrens') incomes in order to keep up with others and maintain their relative position in an ever more affluent society, they must accumulate further assets and expand their businesses, which again sets them apart from wage and salary earners, who acquire a share in society's rising standard of living more or less automatically and need to invest at the most in additional training.

These are tentative observations on the capitalist's attitude to asset holdings, presented in the absence of a systematic theory comparable to Modigliani's theory of the wage and salary earner's behavior. They accord well with the now emerging new theory of corporate behavior —and the corporation is the main capitalist of modern times. The simple classic theory of the firm as a profit maximizer is increasingly rejected as inadequate; instead, the motivation of corporate management is conveived of in terms of at least two competing aims: the growth of the firm and another aim variously defined as dividends, financial security, or retention of control. Those writers who visualize management as integrating the two aims do so by assuming that it maximizes the firm's rate of growth out of undistributed profits, subject to the constraint of keeping dividends at a level adequate to maintain the market value of the corporate stock or to keep stockholders satisfied with management, or adequate by some other standard.[12] All this implies that corporate saving is not dampened by the accumulation of assets, except in one sense. If the growth of the firm creates economies of scale, the ratio of its assets to income falls and the constraint of keeping distributed earnings constant in relation to assets enables the firm to save and plough back profits into further growth at a faster rate. Conversely, if growth creates diseconomies, it raises the assets-to-income ratio and leads, with an unchanged rate of

[11]See, however, the next paragraph.

[12]Cf. W. J. Baumol, *Business Behavior, Value and Growth,* (Macmillan, New York, 1959); R. Marris, *The Economic Theory of Managerial Capitalism,* (Macmillan & Co., London, 1964); and E. T. Penrose, *The Theory of the Growth of the Firm,* (Wiley, New York, 1959).

distributed earnings, to a slower rate of corporate saving and growth. Here, then, is an implication of the modern theories of the firm that is akin and similar to the Pigou effect, though very different in motivation.

As to capitalists other than the corporation, it is worth at least mentioning Modigliani's attempt to extend his life-cycle hypothesis to them also. He assumes that where there are capitalists who, instead of spending their accumulated assets, leave them to their children, there are also capitalists' children and grandchildren who live high off inherited wealth and end, if not in the poorhouse, at least without leaving inheritance. In other words, side by side with ordinary people, who accumulate savings and spend their accumulation within a single life-time, Modigliani assumes the existence of "chains of capitalists" who go through the same cycle more slowly, spread over successive generations, with father and son, or grandfather and grandson, dividing between them the labor of accumulation and decumulation.

There remains the question of the relative importance of capitalists and wage and salary earners in determining the behavior of the entire economy. To answer this, one must note that the coefficients and ratios obtained by fitting equation (1) to U.S. data already show the behavior characteristics of an economy composed of both types of decision makers. The corresponding coefficients and ratios obtained from Modigliani's synthetic model containing solely wage and salary earners showed a marginal propensity to consume out of assets twice, and an asset-to-income ratio half as great. The discrepancy may be taken as a measure of the influence of corporate and capitalist behavior in the economy.

On the other hand, Modigliani's empirical results are still very tentative. They will need more confirmation and the entire subject much more empirical work before real credence can be given to numerical findings. In the meantime, we shall use Modigliani's coefficients for illustrative purposes. The only assumption crucial for some of the arguments that follow is that the size of asset holdings has a positive influence on the propensity to consume out of given income.

The existence of a positive asset effect implies the existence also of a desired or equilibrium asset-to-income ratio. For the U.S. economy, Modigliani obtained a value of about 4½ for this ratio; but there may be great differences in this ratio between different economies.

We shall try to explain some riddles and resolve some problems by tentatively assuming such differences. In Modigliani's world, differences in the number of children and in life- and earning-span expectancies will explain such differences. Other, and perhaps more important explanations, may be the different importance of capitalists and capitalists' savings in different economies, and differences in institutions and social habits. It is very likely, for example, that poor and underdeveloped economies should have a much lower desired asset-to-income ratio than rich and developed countries. Poverty enforces a hand-to-mouth existence, causing people either to work until they drop dead or to rely on their children to feed and house them in their old age. Modigliani's prudent asset holders are creatures of an affluent bourgeois economy.

Bibliography to Chapter 2

There is virtually no explicit theory of the demand and supply of assets; most of it forms part of the modern theories of the consumption function. In this field, Milton Friedman's work (especially his *A Theory of the Consumption Function*) and Franco Modigliani's is the most important. For general reviews of the subject, see M. J. Farrell, "The New Theories of the Consumption Function," *Economic Journal,* Vol. 69 (1959) pp. 678–696 and H. Houthakker, "The Present State of Consumption Theory: A Survey Article," *Econometrica,* Vol. 29 (1961) pp. 704–40. This chapter is based on Modigliani's work, as listed in footnote 6 on p. 17, primarily because the demand for holding assets and the role of asset holdings as a determinant of consumption are more clearly and explicitly stated in his presentation. The subject has a tremendous and fast-growing literature. for which see section 2.315 of the *Index of Economic Journals.*

Chapter 3

The creation of money

In the last chapter we discussed the nature of assets and the public demand for holding them; but nothing has been said so far on how the total supply of assets and their rate of accumulation are determined. The creation of the national debt is, of course, a matter of economic policy, and so not amenable to this kind of analysis. The creation and accumulation of real assets, however, depend among other things on interest rates and credit conditions; and these in turn are determined by the relation between the pattern of supply and the pattern of demand for financial assets of different degrees of liquidity. This is the subject matter of the present chapter.

A. FINANCIAL ASSETS AND THEIR MARKETS

The production of goods and services generates income, of which a part is consumed, a part saved. Both parts have their counterpart among the goods and services whose production generates the income: they correspond to consumption goods and services and to investment goods respectively. For the income to be generated, the goods must be produced, which in turn hinges on the presence of effective demand to stimulate their production. The way in which the desire to consume creates effective demand for consumers' goods and so stimulates their production is simple and direct. Not nearly so simple or direct is the connection between the desire to save and the amount actually saved. The desire to save must create or coincide with effective demand for investment goods if the saving is to be performed. In other words, for a saving decision to create savings, there must be a parallel decision to create investment. And the market cannot be relied upon always and automatically to transmute saving decisions into investment decisions.

If the people and firms who saved part of their income would themselves invest this saving into durable goods, equipment, and construction, there would be no problem. The very act of saving would generate effective demand for investment goods. Indeed, a part of society's saving is invested in precisely this way. Consumers do invest in homes and consumers' durables; businessmen and firms do plough back part of their profits into business expansion. The greater part of saving, however, goes through the market and is invested by others rather than by the savers themselves. Every market transaction whereby a saver hands over savings to an investor creates a financial asset, issued by the investor and acquired by the saver. The financial assets issued by the person or firm that makes the investment in real assets are called primary securities or primary financial assets. The rate at which primary securities accumulate measures the volume of saving invested through the market. Its ratio to the economy's total flow of saving (the rate of accumulation of real assets) measures the extent to which investors invest other people's saving—i.e., saving other than their own.

This points to a potential pitfall of the capitalist economy. People who entrust their saving to others to invest usually want assurance of getting all of it back again, and seek part of this assurance in the safety margin created by the investors' own assets. The primary financial assets are usually secured by the real assets into which the proceeds are invested; and in order to be protected against a possible fall in the latter's market value, the buyer of the financial assets will insist that the real assets backing them be worth more than what he paid for the financial assets. This is why the investor needs "seed money," his own saving to invest together with borrowed saving. And the investor's own saving must stand in a certain minimum proportion to borrowed saving to satisfy the lender's demand for safety.

For investment to be possible therefore, a minimum proportion of it must be saved by the investor himself. If he saves less, the amount he can borrow will be smaller in proportion and so will be his total investment; and with investment lower, income as well as saving will also be lower.

This kind of problem is often mentioned in connection with consumers' investment in housing and consumers' durables. They need mortgages and instalment credit to make such investment; but if their own savings are too small for the down-payments required, this will limit their effective demand both for credit and for consumers' investment. Those anxious to maintain full-employment output by stimulating housing construction and durable-goods production often advocate in such cases the easing of down-payment requirements. But the borrowing of too high a percentage of consumers' investment, even if acceptable to lenders, carries dangers. It increases the percentage of defaults and lenders' losses from defaults, and therewith the danger of precipitating a crisis of confidence. Hence the fears when the volume of mortgages and instalment credit rises fast or reaches high levels, although the crucial magnitude is the ratio of credit to the total investment it helps to finance.

Businessmen are usually in a better position to borrow than consumers. They often have unencumbered assets they can pledge as security against the newly issued financial assets and in such cases do not have to have own saving to invest side-by-side with borrowed saving. It remains true that in our type of economy, a part of investment must be investment of the investor's own savings, because without this, other people's saving cannot be secured and will not be generated. The investor's own saving, however, need not be performed at the same time as the borrowed saving, it can also consist of the accumulation of his past savings.

A certain amount of saving performed and ploughed back by the investor himself therefore is one condition for the proper functioning of the market that transmits saving from saver to investor. A second condition is that the financial assets created in the process be acceptable to both savers and investors, offering sufficiently attractive advantages to the former and not too onerous obligations for the latter. These two conditions, though quite different in nature, are closely related to each other. Success in meeting the second makes it easier to meet the first, because the greater the safety and convenience that financial assets offer to the lender, the smaller the safety margin he will require in the form of the investor's own equity.

The means whereby the market can better fulfil the second condition and also control the flow of saving from savers to investors is the creation of secondary financial assets or indirect securities. While primary securities are issued by investors or ultimate borrowers against the security of real assets, indirect securities are issued by financial intermediaries against the security of primary (or other secondary) financial assets. The mere issuing of indirect securities therefore leaves unchanged the net value of all financial assets, except for its influence on asset prices. Indirect securities differ from the securities against which they are issued in that they usually offer more convenience but less yield. The added convenience is mostly that of greater liquidity or lesser risk; and the most important indirect security is money.

If it were not for the existence of indirect securities, the asset market would be indistinguishable from any other market in its functions and mode of operation. If primary securities were the only financial assets, the person who performed the saving would always hold the same assets that were issued by the person who performed the investment and would so receive for his savings exactly the same "commodity" that the investor gave for them. In this case, the market would merely perform the ordinary functions of all markets: bring the parties together, see to it that market transactions were put into legally enforceable form, make known the terms of previous transactions to create a uniform, competitive price, and remunerate the middleman for his services.

It is the presence of indirect securities that gives the asset market its unique position and influence over the level of investment. These securities offer their holders more liquidity or less risk than the primary securities on which they are based, which means that the savers who hold them enjoy a convenience created, not by the investors who use their savings, but by the financial intermediaries who issued the secondary assets. The larger the quantity of these assets, the greater the liquidity or the freedom from risk enjoyed by savers, and the more favorable the terms on which they are willing to make their savings available. The market forces the intermediaries to pass on at least part of this improvement in terms to the investors; and their investment and demand for savings will be the greater, the more favorable these terms. In short, changes in the quantity of indirect securities can change the prices of primary securities and with them the cost of savings to investors, which in turn is a determinant of the level of investment and saving. This is why control or partial control over the supply of indirect securities carries with it influence over investment and the general level of economic activity, income, and employment.

A financial intermediary is not a simple middleman, because the indirect securities he issues are qualitatively different from the primary securities on which they are based. It is best to think of him as a manufacturer whose output is the indirect securities he issues, and whose main (but not only) inputs are the primary securities he buys. He can make a profit, because he offers a convenience to savers, investors, or both, the demand for which would be unfilled or insufficiently filled without him. If he were a monopolist able to practice discriminating monopoly, he could arrogate to himself the entire benefit of the gain his services create, and his entry into the asset market would make no change other than to provide him with a livelihood.

This, however, is clearly a limiting and unlikely case. Competition causes the actions of most economic agents to confer benefits also on others and to create consumers' and producers' surpluses as these benefits are called. Financial intermediaries are no exception. Their activity usually benefits the savers and probably affects their propensity to save; and above all, it also benefits investors and so influences the level of investment, income, and saving.

Benefits accrue to savers in the form of lesser risk or greater liquidity not fully offset by the loss of interest received. Whether and how this affects the amount saved out of given income is hard to tell, because very little is known about the way in which the reward for saving influences the propensity to save. Higher interest enables one to obtain the same future income for less saving but may raise the demand for future income; and on balance, the propensity to save may either rise or fall with the interest rate. What little evidence is available suggests that it is more likely to rise; but this evidence is too meagre and far from conclusive.

The influence of financial intermediaries on the propensity to save may be a little easier to predict. For financial intermediation increases the return on saving in the form, not of higher interest, but of less risk and more liquidity; and these render saving more attractive without much reducing the need for it. Hence the conjecture that financial intermediation stimulates the propensity to save.[1]

It is, however, through the benefit conferred on investors and the difference this makes to their investment decisions that the operations of financial intermediaries exert their main influence on the economy. The greater the proportion of indirect securities in the public's total asset holdings, the more fully its demand for liquidity and insurance against risk is satisfied; and this increases the availability and lowers the terms of credit to investors in two ways. First, a large proportion of liquid and/or riskless assets in people's portfolios makes them more willing to bear risk on the balance of their portfolios. Second, since the issuers of indirect securities obtain part of the public's savings at a much lower interest cost than would need to be paid if no liquidity or insurance against risk were provided, they are in a position to relend such savings to investors on better terms than these could get by borrowing directly from the saving public. It is not to their advantage to do so; but competition among financial intermediaries in the markets where they lend forces them to; and the lower the terms offered to investors, the more they will borrow and invest. The nature of indirect securities and the importance of each type in their total also influence the terms on which investors can borrow; but an increase in the quantity of any one or any combination of indirect securities will usually lower these terms, stimulate investment, and raise the level of economic activity.

B. THE CREATION OF INDIRECT SECURITIES

When a financial intermediary issues and sells to the public its own indirect securities backed by primary securities it buys, its operation can be regarded as a resale of the primary securities with an insurance policy attached and insurance fee added (or deducted). This interpretation is obvious in the case of investment companies. The indirect securities they issue, called mutual funds, give title to a proportionate share of the company's holdings of primary corporate stock. The

[1]Cf. W. Fellner, *Probability and Profit* (Irwin, 1965, Homewood, Ill.), p. 133.

owner of such mutual funds holds, by proxy, a more diversified and better selected portfolio of primary securities than he would be able, in view of his lesser expertise and the smallness of his own funds, to hold directly. He benefits from the lesser risk better spread but pays the cost of management and the managers' salaries.

The effect of these intermediaries on investment is to raise the demand for corporate stock and hence their prices, and also to inject a dose of discriminatory expertise into the stock market. Their impact in the United States is perhaps not very great; but in India for example, the Government established Unit Trust, a public corporation, specifically to encourage private saving and stimulate private investment.

A very similar function is performed by life insurance companies when they sell their policies and buy primary securities with the proceeds, except that their activity stimulates demand and lowers interest rates mainly in the markets for mortgages and bonds rather than in that for corporate stock.

Somewhat different is the nature and more important the impact of financial intermediaries that provide liquidity. Included in this group are the central bank, which issues legal tender, commercial banks, whose customers' deposits are our main form of money; and also such non-bank intermediaries as mutual savings banks, and savings and loan associations, whose customers' deposits are not considered money, but the creation of which nevertheless supplies liquidity and so lowers interest rates and encourages investment.

In a special category is the central bank and for two reasons. First, the moneyness of the assets it issues is assured by the law of the land, which enforces their acceptance in the payment of debt, taxes, and other obligations to pay. Second, the central bank of a country is its monetary authority, whose actions are in the service, not of the pursuit of gain, but of economic policy.

Central-bank money consists of currency in general circulation and of the deposits on its books of commercial banks, the treasury, and a few other selected customers. In the United States, this latter type of central-bank money is called Federal Funds. In the following, we shall always use the word cash to mean both kinds of central-bank money. Against all or most of the cash they issue, central banks hold primary securities: mainly domestic Government debt but partly also gold and other external reserves, which assure the convertibility into foreign moneys of the cash they create. The amount of cash in circulation can be changed by an in- or out-flow of external reserves or by the purchase or sale of domestic primary assets. The first results from the public's wish to buy or sell domestic against foreign money; the second can result from the commercial banks' decision to sell (rediscount) short-term bills, but it mostly happens on the central bank's initiative when it engages in the open market buying or selling of Government debt in order to change the supply of money. For cash is an essential ingredient in the creation of all forms of money and liquidity; and the supply of cash therefore is an important determinant of the supply of all forms of money and liquidity.

The creation of liquidity by all other financial intermediaries is again a form of insurance based on the law of large numbers. Each holder of liquid assets wants the certainty of being able to spend them at a moment's notice when the need arises; but he may have no idea whether or when the need will arise. About a large group of such people, however, it is possible to predict that no more than a fraction of their total liquid assets will be withdrawn and spent, and that of this fraction again only a fraction will be spent outside the group. It is their knowledge of these regularities and of the value of these fractions that enables the financial intermediaries to guarantee the spendability of their assets and yet to make a profit.

If some special convenience or advantage, coupled with the promise of repayment on demand, persuades a group of people to deposit part of their cash or other liquid assets for safekeeping with a financial intermediary, the latter can make good his promise by keeping on hand only a fraction of the deposited assets and make a profit by loaning the rest out on interest. If his customers consider their deposit slips as good as the assets deposited, they (the deposit slips) become an additional supply of liquid assets as a result. This follows from the principle of consumers' sovereignty. Whatever the public considers as good as money, becomes thereby as good as money and the economist must accept it as an addition to the supply of money. Moreover, if part of the assets loaned out by the financial intermediary are again deposited, this further increases the supply of liquid assets, until the total increase becomes a multiple of the original assets deposited.

The financial intermediary's interest earnings are the greater, the more of the assets deposited he lends out; but if he retains insufficient reserves, the need to make good his promise may force him to borrow at interest or sell some of his interest-bearing assets at a possible capital loss, incurring a cost in either case. The balancing of revenues on loans and other interest-bearing assets against the expected cost of borrowing or forced sales determines the most profitable ratio of reserves to deposits. Since this ratio also determines the contribution to liquidity that the entry and operation of a financial intermediary will make, it is quite important for our analysis.

Among the factors that influence a financial intermediary's most profitable ratio of reserves to deposits are the habits and preferences of his depositors, and the stability of their habits and preferences with respect both to their spending behavior, and to their choice of different assets to hold. Another factor is the number, nature, and importance of other financial intermediaries in the economy. Also, the monetary authority has power in most advanced countries to influence the deposit banks' profit-maximizing ratio of reserves to deposits by prescribing a minimum ratio and imposing a punitive interest charge on banks whose reserve ratio falls below this minimum. As long as this exceeds the banks' calculation of their most profitable reserve ratio without the punitive interest charge, the prescribing and occasional changing of this minimum reserve ratio is an effective tool of monetary policy.

It will be useful for what follows, to spell out in detail the way in which and extent to which the action of financial intermediaries creates liquidity. We shall use as our example the creation of demand deposits by the commercial banks, since they are the most important indirect security and the main form of money in our economy.

What is the amount of money a banker creates when he maintains a reserve ratio q between cash and customers' deposits, faces people willing to deposit with him a proportion p of the money they hold, and the stock of cash in circulation is Q? The banker himself is conscious, not of creating money, but of receiving on deposit pQ of the public's cash holdings and lending out a fraction $(1 - q)$ of it. Money is created nevertheless; because in his effort to attract depositors, he has made deposits so attractive to them, and so easily convertible into cash, that his customers never think of themselves as parting with money when they make a deposit. They regard the operation as changing merely the form but *not* the quantity of the money they hold. This is why the loan of $(1 - q)pQ$ made by the bank does create money and does represent a net addition to the total stock of money held. Furthermore, since the loan is made in cash, a proportion p of the loan will again be deposited with the bank, enabling it to lend out a fraction $(1 - q)$ of this further deposit, and thus to create an additional $(1 - q)^2p^2Q$ of money. Continuing this process brings the total of money in the hands of the public to:

$$M = [1 + (1 - q)p + (1 - q)^2p^2 + \ldots] Q = \frac{Q}{1 - (1 - q)p}.^{2}$$

When there are n deposit banks, of which the jth maintains a reserve ratio q_j and receives on deposit a fraction p_j of the public's total holdings of money, the total amount of money is given by the expression:

$$M = \frac{Q}{1 - \Sigma (1 - q_j)q_j}.$$

Since the several banks in the same economy usually maintain the same reserve ratio, q, the above expression can be simplified to:

(1)
$$M = \frac{Q}{1 - (1 - q) \ \Sigma p_j},$$

where $\sum_{j=1}^{m} p_j$ is the proportion of its money holdings the public chooses to hold on deposit with banks in general.

The above expressions show, M, the total amount of money (i.e., cash and bank deposits) created given the amount of cash, Q; and they show M to be a multiple of Q, considering that the q's, the p's, and Σp are all positive fractions. In the United States at the end of 1966, equation (1) had the following value:

$$\$169 \text{ bil.} = \frac{\$61.2 \text{ bil.}}{1 - (1 - .18).78}.$$

The ratio of M to Q (2.8 in the above equation) is sometimes called the credit multiplier. It shows the leverage with which the monetary authority can, by changing Q, the supply of money it creates, induce a change in M, the total quantity of money in the hands of the public. As already mentioned, the monetary authority can also change M by changing q, the banks' reserve ratio.

[2]The series converges, since both p and q are positive fractions smaller than one.

The establishment of an $(n + 1)$th deposit bank, offering customers the same facilities and maintaining (or compelled by the monetary authority to maintain) the same reserve ratio as the other n banks, would not add to the quantity of money, because its establishment would not raise Σp, the proportion of money the public holds on deposit with banks in general. All that would happen is that people who found the new bank more convenient to deal with would transfer to it their deposits from other banks, forcing a proportional transfer also of cash, but leaving the sum total of all deposits unchanged.

The situation is slightly different when this $(n + 1)$th deposit bank offers a convenience not previously available. It may be the first bank, for example, in a small community, and its establishment may change people's banking habits in this community, causing them to use less cash and more checks than they used before. In this case, the value of Σp for the economy as a whole will be raised and will raise the value of M with unchanged Q. However, the local cash that will now be banked is not likely to stay in the new bank and serve as the base for multiple credit expansion by this bank alone. For, as the bank grants its first loans, much of their proceeds will be spent in other communities, add to the reserves of other banks, and enable these (rather than the first bank) to extend further loans. Credit expansion is always shared by all the deposit banks in the same economy, with the loans granted by one raising the reserves of all.

It appears, then, that apart from the limited extent to which the public is likely to change the proportions in which it holds cash and bank deposits, the latter's supply is closely linked to that of cash and can only change in response to the central bank's changing either the supply of cash or the deposit banks' minimum reserve requirements.

We have been concerned so far with cash (central-bank money) on the one hand and deposit money (demand deposits in commercial banks) on the other hand, the two together constituting what is usually called money. There are, however, other forms of money and many other forms of liquidity, over whose supply the central bank has very much less influence. This is so, partly because the public's use of them is more flexible and subject to change, partly because their issuance, mostly, is not subject to legal reserve requirements. Travelers' checks, for example, and the overdraft facilities available to holders of credit cards are clearly forms of money;[3] but they are

[3]E.g., the credit cards issued by California's Bank of America (Bankamericard)

too new as yet, and too unimportant, for their supply to be regulated by law and controlled by monetary authority.

Much more important quantitatively are savings deposits in commercial banks, mutual savings banks, and in savings and loan associations; as well as the Certificates of Deposit issued by commercial banks, a kind of savings deposit specially tailored to fit the convenience of large firms. Savings deposits in commercial banks are recognized by the authorities as almost money (quasi money). Their quantity is under central-bank control in much the same way as the quantity of demand deposits: it is subject to similar, though very much lower, minimum reserve requirements.[4] The Federal Reserve Banks have no such control over the quantity of savings deposits in mutual savings banks and savings and loan associations. In actual fact, the ratio of reserves they hold against customers' deposits is very similar to the ratio of reserves the commercial banks hold against their savings deposits; but the Federal Reserve Banks cannot set and enforce minimum reserve requirements. Also, and this is by far the more important point, mutual savings banks and savings and loan associations are not required to, and do not hold their reserves in central-bank money, *Q;* but hold them instead in what the public regards as money, *M;* that is, partly in cash, partly in commercial-bank demand deposits. In other words, just as commercial-bank deposits (both demand and savings deposits) are pyramided on cash, so savings-bank deposits are pyramided on commercial-bank demand deposits and cash, and thus constitute another layer in this hierarchical system of moneys. This means that there is much scope for savings banks to create deposits in addition to those created by the commercial banks, because when they create savings deposits, they divert virtually no cash reserves from the commercial banks and do not force them to make an offsetting reduction in the deposits they create.

give, at the time of writing, their 2.3 million holders a total credit limit of over $500 million, of which on the average about $300 million are unused. From the customer's point of view, such unused credit is as good as money in the bank. In England, Australia and New Zealand, it is customery and legal for banks to let the owners of ordinary checking accounts overdraw their accounts. In New Zealand, the only country that publishes statistics on the volume of unused overdraft facilities, these amount to almost half as much as the volume of money — and they are as good as money and require no reserves at all.

[4]The minimum requirement of cash reserves against savings deposits is usually around one third to one fourth the required reserve ratio against demand deposits.

At the same time, the public makes virtually no distinction between savings deposits in savings banks and those in commercial banks; and it regards all savings deposits as only a very little less liquid than demand deposits. Therefore, the creation of savings deposits has very much the same effect as the creation of demand deposits. It provides additional liquidity to the public and so encourages investment; and it probably also increases the propensity to save.

Just to give an idea of the orders of magnitude involved, it is worth noting that at the end of 1966 in the United States, when of $61.2 billion cash in circulation (currency and Federal Funds) the public (other than the commercial banks) held $37.3 billion, which, together with $131.7 billion demand deposits, formed a total of $169 billion of money in the hands of the public; savings deposits in commercial banks amounted to $155.2 billion, in savings institutions to $166 billion, adding up to a total of $321 billion of what is sometimes called quasi money. Money and quasi money together constitute the bulk of the indirect securities that provide liquidity in our economy.

We mentioned earlier that the creation of liquidity by commercial banks and other financial intermediaries is a form of insurance. Bankers count on not every depositor wanting to spend all his money at the same time, and on stability in the proportion of money they will want to spend at any time. This enables them to issue many more promises to pay cash (which is what deposits are) than the amount of cash they have on reserve; and it explains, for the economy as a whole, the pyramiding of a large volume of money on a much smaller volume of cash. A bank balance can be regarded as an insurance policy against the danger of wanting to spend cash; and it is normal for the value of all the policies issued by insurance companies to exceed the value of their assets.

The probability, however, on whose basis the banks insure their customers against the danger of wanting to spend their money is very different in kind from the probability of the accidents that insurance companies insure against. The latter are independent random events with a predictable frequency in a large population. This is true of most natural accidents and of those human accidents which the people to whom they might happen are anxious to avoid. Some accidents are not independent events, such as epidemic deaths or fires in dry areas; and insurance companies will insure against these only if they can reinsure with reinsurance companies large enough to regard an entire epidemic as a single (and independent) event in a population of epidemics. Accidents interdependent on too large a scale even for reinsurance companies to handle cannot, as a rule, be insured against. Hence the exclusion of damage from war in most insurance policies.

The dangers a banker insures against, depositors' withdrawing money, are independent random events as long, but only as long as depositors have full confidence that their demands for cash will be met. The moment such confidence is shaken for reasons good or bad, real or imaginary, loss of confidence spreads like a contagion; and then nothing can prevent a run on the bank, and nothing but 100 per cent reserves its bankruptcy. Neither can a probability calculation predict the frequency of such an event.

Here, too, reinsurance is the solution,[5] important not only because banks provide a service useful to their customers, but even more so because stable credit conditions and a stable volume of money are vital for the proper functioning of the economy. In the United States, reinsurance is provided by the insurance, up to $15,000, of bank deposits with the Federal Deposit Insurance Corp., of savings-bank deposits with the Federal Savings and Loan Insurance Corp.; and by the role of the Federal Reserve Banks as lenders of last resort. These can supplement the reserves of commercial banks in many ways and are expected to do so generously in an emergency.

Bibliography to Chapter 3

On the nature and functions of primary and secondary assets and financial intermediation, see John J. Gurley and Edward S. Shaw, *Money in a Theory of Finance* (Brookings, 1960), also their "Financial Aspects of Economic Development", *American Economic Review*, Vol. 45 (1955) pp. 515–38; and Don Patinkin, "Financial Intermediaries and Monetary Theory", *American Economic Review*, Vol. 51 (1961) pp. 95–116.

On liquidity creation by banks, see Karl Brunner, "A Schema for the Supply Theory of Money", *International Economic Review*, Vol. 2 (1961) pp. 79–109.

[5]A policy of exclusions would destroy the very concept of liquidity.

Chapter 4

The preference for money

It was argued in chapter 2 that people's motive for holding assets is their wish to reduce the dependence of the time shape of their expenditures on the time shape of their revenues. One motive, and perhaps the main one for holding money is very similar. Money is the most readily spendable asset, hence it is the best one to hold for bridging the more short-run discrepancies between the time shape of revenues and the desired time-shape of expenditures. This is known as the transactions motive for holding money. A second, the precautionary motive for holding money, is to reduce fluctuations in, and the unpredictability of the market value of one's total asset holdings. This will be shown also to be a short-run consideration. A third, the speculative motive, is somewhat different and accounts for occasional and temporary demand for money in response to expected changes in asset values and with a view to maximizing the value (or growth of the value) of one's asset position. We proceed to discuss each of these in turn.

A. THE TRANSACTIONS MOTIVE

Early thinking on why people hold money concentrated on differences in the spacing and timing of day-to-day receipts and expenditures. The early writers on the quantity theory of money had a very mechanical conception of the magnitude of this demand. It seemed self-evident to them that the demand for holding money would be proportional to the volume of transactions—the inflow and outflow of payments—and that the proportionality ratio depended on such factors as the degree of differentiation between industries and the socially customary intervals at which wages and salaries were received, bills paid, financial transactions settled. All these are stable factors; not likely to change, except gradually, through time. Hence the assertions in this early quantity theory, which considered the transactions motive the only motive for holding money, that the demand for money is proportional to the volume of transactions and the level of income.[1]

Only the economists following Keynes realized that assets other than money can also perform, if not quite so well, this bridging function between the different patterns of the flow of receipts and the flow of expenditures; this is why they introduced the rate of interest on other assets as yet another determinant of the ratio in which people want to hold money in relation to their incomes and expenditures. Since interest is an advantage of other assets which counterbalances the advantage that its greater liquidity imparts to money; the higher the rate of interest, the more anxious is the public to economize in its use of money and the more willing to put up with the inconvenience of occasionally using other assets where money would be more convenient.

The next step, taken by Baumol and Tobin,[2] was to challenge the assumption of proportionality and apply the theory of inventory holdings to the holding of money. The transactions demand for holding *assets* may well be proportional to the flow of transactions or income,

[1]The earlier writers speak of volume of transactions; later ones, preferring to this somewhat nebulous concept a more tangible one, have substituted the level of income — assuming, perhaps too cavalierly, proportionality between the two.

[2]Cf. W. J. Baumol, "The Transactions Demand for Cash: An Inventory Theoretic Approach" *Quarterly Journal of Economics*, Vol. 66 (1952) pp. 545–56; J. Tobin, "The Interest Elasticity of Transactions Demand for Cash", *Review of Economics and Statistics*, Vol. 38 (1956) pp. 241–47.

but the part of such assets held in the form of money is probably a function of the interest rate; and the form of this function and the nature of the relation of money holdings to the flow of transactions can be derived from the assumption that holders of money wish to minimize the costs incurred in holding money.

The holding of money involves the cost of foregoing the interest that other assets would earn; and this cost increases (usually in proportion) with the size of money holdings. In addition, the acquiring of money preliminary to spending it also involves a cost—the brokerage fee, commission, and bother of selling earning assets and so converting them into money. This cost depends largely on the frequency with which such conversions are made and so diminishes with the size of one's money holdings. If a person's annual volume of payments is T, and the sum he customarily converts from earning assets into money is C, then the number of such conversions is T/C and their annual cost is $\frac{T}{C}(b + kC)$—assuming the cost of each conversion to be a linear fuction $(b + kC)$ of the sum converted. The average size of this person's money holding is $\frac{C}{2}$, and the annual interest foregone on it is $i\frac{C}{2}$, where i is the market rate of interest. His total annual cost therefore of holding money is

$$K = \frac{T}{C}(b + kC) + i\frac{C}{2}.$$

By equating to zero the derivative of this function with respect to C, Baumol obtains the value of C that minimizes the total cost of holding money:

$$C = \sqrt{\frac{2bT}{i}}\ .$$

This result is familiar from inventory analysis where it has also been borne out empirically; and it suggests that the demand for holding money increases in proportion, not with the volume of transactions, but with its square root.

So far, empirical studies have not confirmed this theoretical expectation. No study of householders' holdings of money has yet been made to test the hypothesis; a cross-section study according to size (volume of transactions) of business firms' holdings of money shows proportionality; and it is hard to tell how far this is explained by such offsetting factors as the lower interest rates payable by large firms, the greater importance to them of the prestige conferred by large bank balances, or possibly the nature and importance of the precautionary motive.[3]

B. THE PRECAUTIONARY MOTIVE

An asset whose worth at a given future date is known with certainty to be X, and another whose worth at the same date is uncertain but the mathematical expectation of whose uncertain future value is also X (owing to equal probabilities attached to the chances of its having a higher and a correspondingly lower value) are not equally valuable to the consumer. People who value certainty and predictability will prefer the first—they might do so even if its certain value were somewhat lower than the expected value of the second. Here then is a further motive for preferring money to other assets, different from the transactions motive and possibly explaining a demand for holding money beyond the latter's requirements.

There arise, however, a number of complications. To begin with, not everybody prefers certainty to uncertainty. Some people are gamblers; and the very concept of a precautionary motive makes no sense as far as they are concerned. Secondly, a preference for certainty and predictability need not always imply a preference for money over other assets. Uncertainty, of the kind discussed here, stems from the need to buy or sell assets at uncertain future market prices. To minimize uncertainty therefore, this need must be minimized; and the holding of money will not always minimize it for everybody. People, for example, whose need to spend accumulated purchasing power is spread evenly over a long period of time (e.g., widows and orphans) have a desired expenditure pattern (or one prescribed by dead husbands or parents), whose time shape can be closely matched by the payments promised and made on dividend-

[3]Cf. A. H. Meltzer, "The Demand for Money: A Cross-Section Study of Business Firms," "*Quarterly Journal of Economics*, Vol. 77 (1963) pp. 405–22. This study, however, relates the demand for holding money not to the interest rate *earned* but to that *paid* by firms.

and interest-bearing securities. Others whose need to spend is deferred for a known period can either match this by holding assets redeemable after the same period; or, if the period is long, they can best insure against the uncertainties of the future by holding equities. If any of these people held money instead, their financial position would either be worse (money having no yield) without being more secure, or (if they planned to buy securities later) be subject to more instead of less uncertainty.

The holding of money instead of other assets diminishes risk only for those concerned over uncertainty in the short run, for people who want to be ready at short notice and at a near but unpredictable future date to pick up a bargain, seize the opportunity of an especially favorable investment, or rise to an emergency that requires expenditure. For them, uncertainty is reduced the more, the greater the proportion of their assets held in the form of money; although this also reduces the expected yield of their total asset holdings.

It appears therefore that the yield of one's total assets and the predictability of their value in the near future are alternatives. They can be combined in varying proportions by trading one for the other through changing the proportion of money in one's total portfolio of assets.

The precautionary motive for holding money increases, first of all, with the total volume of a person's assets, considering that the riskiness of his asset position depends on the *proportion* of assets held in the form of money. Secondly, it increases as the market rate of interest falls, for reasons best analyzed in terms of an indifference map, developed by Tobin, which shows the individual's preference between average expected yield and the predictability of this yield. Defining the yield of an asset or collection of assets as the sum of its interest- or dividend-yield and the change in its market value, he obtains a probability distribution of the different yields that this asset or collection of assets might be expected to have at a given future date. The mean of this distribution represents the asset holder's expected yield, its standard deviation is assumed to be considered by him to measure the risk involved.

In a plane where the axes measure the mean and the standard deviation of the yield of a person's total portfolio of all assets (including money), movement along a budget line shows the way in which this person can trade freedom from risk against expected yield by varying the proportion of money in his total asset holdings. The person's preferences can be represented by an indifference map, whose shape will be as shown for a "normal" person, with an aversion for the uncertainty of the market value of his assets in the short run.

A change in interest rates changes, first of all, the slope of the budget line, whose effect on a person's preference for money can be analyzed along the lines of the effect of a price change on the consumer's market demand. The substitution effect of a rise in interest rates (assumed to leave unchanged the degree of risk) makes people substitute yield for predictability by reducing the proportion of money in their asset holdings. Geometrically, the rise in interest rates renders the budget line steeper in the diagram; and the substitution effect is a movement along the indifference curve to a point of steeper tangency. The rise in interest rates also raises interest income, whose effect (the income effect) goes in the opposite direction; for a higher income enables a person to have more of both yield *and* predictability. This effect, however, is usually very small, because the higher interest (and dividend) income usually accrues *only on newly acquired securities,* added to the existing stock either by a net saver or by a person who in response to the rise in interest rates reduces his money holdings and adds to his holdings of earning assets. In terms of geometry again, a rise in market rates of interest means getting onto a steeper budget line; but not onto a much higher one. One might show a rise in market rates of interest by swinging the budget line around the point that represents the wealth holder's original combination of yield and predictability.

The income from a person's past accumulation of securities may remain wholly or partly unaffected by the rise in interest rates, depending on the nature of the securities, and also of the interest-rate change. The yield of fixed-interest bearing securities obviously remains unchanged by a rise in market rates of interest, which cause instead a fall in the market value of these securities. This has a wealth effect, which pulls in the opposite direction from the income effect and reinforces the substitution effect. For it makes the owner of the securities feel poorer and hence less able to afford security from risk and the luxury of holding money—all the more so, because the wealth effect reduces not only the total market value of all his assets but the proportion in this total of the value of his interest-bearing securities as well. Hence, with substitution and wealth effects pulling in one direction and only the weak income effect pulling in the other, a rise in interest rates is very likely to reduce the demand for holding money also as far as the precautionary motive is concerned. All this, unfortunately, cannot be represented in Figure 1.

The argument is the same in the case of dividend-bearing securities if the rise in market rates of interest results from a fall in their market value, rather than from a rise in the dividends they pay. Only if the rise in interest rates parallels a rise in dividend payments is the wealth effect absent, and the income effect as important as in the theory of consumer's demand.[3]

All the above analysis applies to "normal" people, with an aversion to risk. Gamblers, having no precautionary motive, are not likely to change their behavior in response to a change in interest rates; widows and orphans, not induced by the precautionary motive to hold money, are not likely to be affected either.

It should be noted that firms, as well as persons, have both a transactions and a precautionary motive for holding money. The transactions motive of firms for having enough money on hand for the prompt payment of wages, salaries, bills, and other obligations arising from the daily conduct of business is self evident. Beyond this, the main, perhaps only motive for firms to hold readily spendable purchasing power is their desire to have their undistributed profits and other funds ready for investment when the time is propitious for expansion or an opportunity arises for buying up another firm. This, however, calls for funds ready, not at a moment's but rather at a month's or two-months' notice; and such funds need not be held in money but can as easily and more profitably be held in interest-bearing assets.

The firm's precautionary motive therefore is a motive for holding financial assets in general, rather than money alone. For firms, other than financial intermediaries, hold assets primarily for the sake of the productive services they yield. This means that they hold mainly real assets, plus money for transaction purposes. It is not worth their while to hold financial assets for their yield, since this is certain

[3]When the rise in dividend payments exceeds the rise in market rates of interest, there is an income *and* a wealth effect pulling in the same direction, opposed to that of the substitution effect.

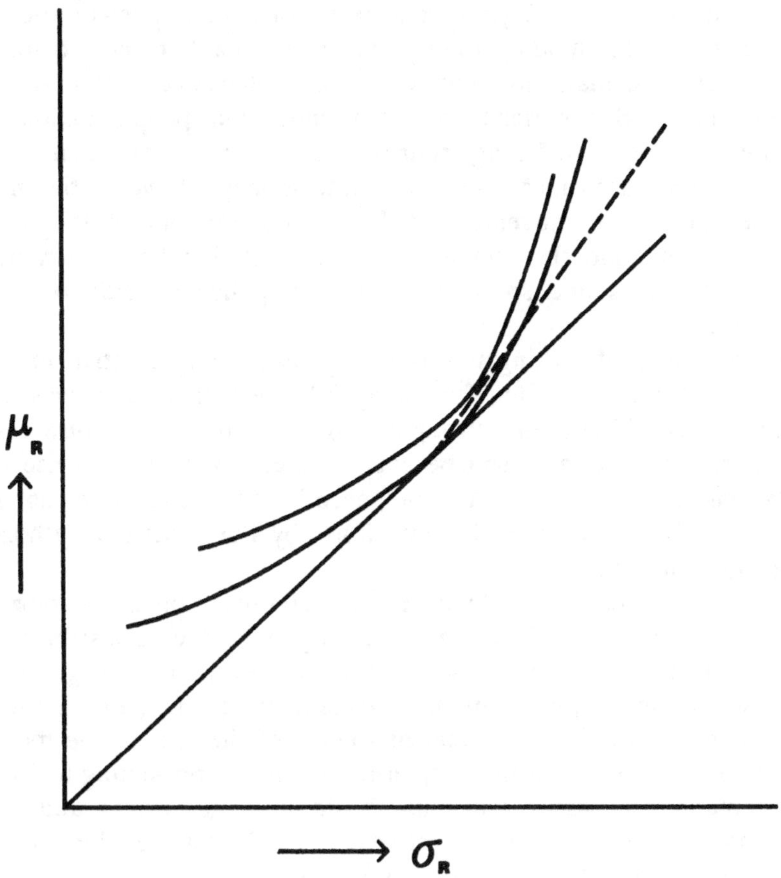

Figure 1

almost always to be much lower than the yield of their investment in the firm itself—except when the financial assets are shares giving controlling interest in another firm. If they nevertheless hold financial assets other than such shares, they do so for the sake of their liquidity.

C. THE SPECULATIVE MOTIVE

A person who expects interest rates to rise and security prices to fall and wants to avoid the resulting capital loss on his holdings of securities has a speculative motive for holding his funds in some form other than securities. Keynes considered this an important though volatile motive for holding money that would explain, not so much the permanent demand for money, as the existence of fluctuations in this demand. U.S. experience, however, shows that people anxious to avoid capital losses in falling security markets tend to put their funds into short-term securities rather than into money. However this may be, the speculative movement of funds into and out of long-term securities can undo the regular and stable relation between money and interest rates and so render monetary policy difficult, or even ineffective.

Another way of putting this is to say that the speculative motive can be a strong and often stabilizing influence on asset prices and interest rates. Widely and strongly held views on what future asset prices and interest rates will be can, if acted upon, make these expectations come true or remain true; even in the face of large changes in the supply of money and great efforts by the monetary authority to change interest rates.

The best known example of the speculative motive's stabilizing effect on interest rates is Keynes' liquidity trap: the impossibility of lowering interest rates below some minimum level, however great the increase in the supply of money. Some writers (including myself) have relied on the interest-stabilizing effect of the speculative motive to explain why a rise in the propensity to save, representing a rise in the demand for assets, will fail to bid up asset prices and thus stimulate investment.[4] But this at best is a subsidiary explanation to the one given in section A of chapter 5 below.

Bibliography to Chapter 4

On the theory of liquidity preference, see J. M. Keynes, *The General Theory of Employment, Interest and Money;* W. J. Baumol, "The Transactions Demand for Cash: An Inventory Theoretic Approach", *Quarterly*

[4]Cf. N. Kaldor: "Speculation and Economic Stability", *Review of Economic Studies,* Vol. 7 (1939) pp. 1–27; T. Scitovsky: "A Study of Interest and Capital", *Economica* N.S. Vol. 7 (1940) pp. 293–317.

Journal of Economics, Vol. 66 (1952) pp. 545–56; J. Tobin, "The Interest Elasticity of the Transactions Demand for Cash", *Review of Economics and Statistics,* Vol. 38 (1956) pp. 241–47; and J. Tobin, "Liquidity Preference as Behavior towards Risk", *Review of Economic Studies,* Vol. 25 (1958) pp. 65–86.

On the empirical verification of the theory, there is a rapidly growing literature for which the reader should consult section 9 of the *Index of Economic Journals,* and of which the Allan Meltzer article cited on p. 41 above is a sample.

Chapter 5

Excess demand and excess supply

An excess demand or excess supply of most commodities will raise or lower price, usually causing demand and supply alike to adjust and help restore equilibrium. When price is not flexible enough to restore equilibrium, the piling up or drawing down of inventories or unfilled orders takes over the function of adjustment, slowing or accelerating the flow of output until equilibrium is restored. Lags and repercussions through other markets can slow, complicate or even vitiate this process of adjustment; but by and large, market forces in commodity markets function fairly well.

In the case of assets held as a store of value, the process of adjustment set in motion by an excess demand or excess supply is altogether different. Its mechanics were first analyzed by Keynes,[1] partly in his theory of the multiplier, partly in his discussion of the demand for and supply of money, whose peculiarities he attributed to its zero elasticity of supply. The nature of this adjustment process, however, does not hinge on this peculiarity of money but is inherent in any adjustment process set in motion by a discrepancy between the stock of assets and the demand for holding them. It will be con-

[1]Cf. J. M. Keynes: *The General Theory of Employment, Interest, and Money.*

venient to deal with discrepancies first between the total stock of all assets and the total demand for holding them, and second between the composition (supply pattern) of different kinds of assets and the pattern of demand for holding them. The main example of this second discrepancy, and the only one to be discussed here, is that between the supply of and demand for liquidity.

A. CHANGES IN THE DEMAND FOR ASSETS: BALANCED EXCESS

Let us recall that an important function of assets, especially of liquid assets, is to facilitate the production of output and income. The division of labor in the productive process necessitates many transactions; and assets, especially liquid assets, are the means of payment in these transactions. They change hands in every transaction—except in some barter transactions. The speed with which the stock of assets, or of a particular type of assets, changes hands is called their velocity of circulation and expressed by the ratio of the annual value of transactions to the value of this stock.

What happens when the community wants to hold more or fewer assets than their existing stock? When a person wants, say, to reduce his asset holdings, all he can do is to spend some of them on goods and services, and in the process transfer these assets to the people who supply the additional goods or services he buys.[2] They in turn may or may not want to keep the assets so acquired. If they do, their additional asset holdings will make them feel more affluent and raise somewhat their permanent spending; if they do not, they will transfer them to yet others for goods and services *they* wish to buy, and this process will continue until the assets come to rest in the hands of people willing to hold them. Whichever happens, the first person's desire to reduce his asset holdings changes the hands in which they are held, raises the velocity with which they change hands, and increases some other people's affluence and propensity to spend. It has left unchanged so far the total stock of assets. The question remains

[2]Throughout the following analysis, we assume the existence of excess productive capacity, so that additional goods and services can be produced without a rise in commodity prices. The assumption will be dropped on p. 53 below.

whether or not the price of assets is changed in the process, and influences their supply; or whether the supply of assets is changed in some other way.

If cash were the only asset held, the answer would obviously be that price is not changed, considering that the price of cash (in terms of money) is fixed at unity and its elasticity of supply is zero. The answer is the same, though not quite so trivial, when both cash and bank deposits are used as assets. One might think at first that by withdrawing money from his account in order to spend it, a customer will lower his bank's reserve ratio and so force it to curtail loans and thus reduce the supply of bank deposits. But this would be true only if the deposit withdrawal resulted from the customer's wish to hold more cash and fewer bank deposits than before. If the ratio in which people wish to hold cash and bank balances remains unchanged and is the same for everybody, a person's wanting to hold fewer assets will reduce his holdings of cash and bank deposits *in equal proportions,* cause a *proportional* increase in someone else's cash holdings and bank deposits, and thus leave completely unchanged the banks' ratio of reserves to customers' deposits. The banks will have no inducement therefore to change their credit policies; and the total supply of cash *and* bank deposits will remain unchanged.

This conclusion is quite general, and can now be extended to the general case where purchasing power is held in the shape of any number and variety of assets. We shall assume that all change in a person's desire or willingness to hold assets is a balanced change, involving proportional changes in his holdings or desired holdings of each type of asset; we shall also assume that everybody holds and wants to hold various assets in the same proportions as everybody else, thus making sure that an interpersonal transfer of assets leaves unchanged the community's desired pattern of asset holdings. As long as we retain these assumptions, it remains true that excess demand or excess supply of assets will affect incomes but leave asset prices unchanged and the supply of assets unaffected, at least through these channels. If a person wants to reduce his asset holdings by ΔA, he spends this much more on goods and services and so causes the people from whom he buys them to find themselves with ΔA additional assets. If he needs money to make his purchases, he must sell other assets to obtain it; but his sale of these assets will, by assumption, be exactly matched, and its effect on asset prices completely offset, by the extra demand for such assets of the people who have now obtained the ΔA additional funds. It appears therefore that in this case, too, a balanced change in the desire to hold assets has no direct impact on asset prices, interest rates, or the supply of assets.

The change will, however, affect the level of incomes. If the people who have now obtained the ΔA additional funds recognize these for a windfall—an addition to their assets but not to their income—they will increase their spending and so set in motion a multiplier process that will raise incomes. The increase in their permanent consumption expenditure will be $a_3 \Delta A$, where a_3 is the marginal propensity to consume out of assets; but of this total only $(a_3 - \alpha r)\, \Delta A$, the part which is over and above what may be considered spending out of the yield, r, of these assets, is a *net* addition to society's total consumption. The rise in incomes due to the multiplier effects of this rise in permanent consumption will be

$$\Delta Y = \frac{a_3 - \alpha r}{1 - \alpha}\, \Delta A,$$

where α is the marginal propensity to consume out of income.

The result is not very different when the recipients of the ΔA additional funds initially mistake their additional receipts for an addition to their permanent income. They will then go on a temporary spending spree, perhaps inducing others to do the same, and so create for a while a much greater rise in spending and output. This will be reversed, however, as soon as people realize their mistakes; and unless the temporary flurry of spending has had a permanent effect on investment, income and spending will settle permanently at the level where it would have settled otherwise: above Y, its previous level, by the amount:

$$\Delta Y = \frac{a_3 - \alpha r}{1 - \alpha}\, \Delta A.$$

This rise in income is occasioned by the excess supply of assets, created in this example by the public's diminished willingness to hold the unchanged stock of assets at unchanged prices. The change in income is the equilibrating force, since it induces the public to hold the undiminished stock of assets despite its diminished propensity to hold them. The equilibrating change in income is probably not very great; the values Modigliani derived for the coefficients from U.S. time-series data yield a multiplier of:

$$\frac{\Delta Y}{\Delta A} = \frac{a_3 - \alpha r}{1 - \alpha} = .14.$$

A $1 billion excess supply of assets would raise incomes by $140 million.

At the same time, with the pattern of demand for holding different types of assets unchanged by assumption, the excess supply of assets leaves unchanged the prices (in terms of money) and hence also the supply of assets. This is so, because, with the price of money fixed at unity, every change in asset prices would be a change in the *relative* prices of different assets, which could only be brought about by a change either in the pattern of demand or in the pattern of supply of different assets.

Our first approximation, then, to a theory of the market in which the accumulated stock of assets is bought and sold by people holding, or desiring to hold them is that an excess supply of assets or an excess demand for holding them will, if it is a balanced excess, leave unchanged the price and hence the stock of assets but exert expansionary or restrictive pressures which bring about equilibrating changes in the level of income. A corollary of this is the familiar Keynesian theorem: a change in the propensity to save affects the level, not of saving, but of income; causing this to change by an amount that will exactly offset the effect on actual saving of the change in the propensity to save.

We assumed so far that the supply of assets remains unchanged, because it can only be changed by investment, which depends on asset prices and interest rates; which in turn were shown to be unaffected by a balanced excess supply or excess demand. But investment also depends, and very greatly, on the level of income, changing in the same direction as this changes. So when an excess supply of assets raises or an excess demand lowers income, it is likely to raise or lower respectively also investment and correspondingly affect the supply of assets. Here then we have a perverse response of the supply of assets to a balanced excess in their supply or demand; and this again is more familiar in its Keynesian form: a fall in the propensity to save is likely to *raise,* and a rise to lower, the actual amount invested and saved.

These paradoxical results, so very different in mechanics and conclusions from what one would expect on the analogy of commodity markets, are hardly modified when we relax the assumption tacitly made so far of constant commodity prices. Though prices are rigid downwards, they may rise in response to the expansionary pressure of an excess supply of assets; and in an inflationary world of secularly rising price levels, even the downward pressure of an excess demand for assets will have an impact by slowing or arresting the secular rise in prices. A change in commodity prices would change the purchasing power represented by a stock of assets unchanged in money value; but this effect will be undone if it also leads to a proportionate change in asset prices, since the change in the money value of assets will offset the change in the purchasing power of money.

Now a change in commodity prices is quite likely to lead to a more or less proportionate change in asset prices. This is obviously true of tangible assets, which are, after all, commodities. The prices of equities will also move with those of the tangible assets to whose ownership they give title. The prices of fixed-interest bearing assets on the other hand will not change; but since many of these are the liabilities of corporations, the value of the stock of these corporations will, as a result, change more than proportionally with the value of the corporation's real assets. In the course of these changes, the structure of asset prices will be distorted; but whether this will slow or speed the creation of new assets is again difficult to predict. In short, dropping the assumption of unchanged commodity prices makes our results more uncertain but does not modify them in a systematic and predictable way.

We must next examine our crucial assumption concerning the unchanged pattern of demand for holding assets. We assumed the initial change to be a change in overall demand, without the pattern of demand also changing; but when a diminished desire to hold assets raises the level of income, it also raises the transactions demand for holding money and so *causes* the pattern of demand for holding assets to change. People's and firms' attempts to adjust their money holdings accordingly will raise interest rates and restrain investment, partly counteracting the effect on incomes of the diminished desire to hold assets. Conversely, an increased desire to hold assets will depress incomes and lower the transactions demand for money; and this change in the pattern of demand for assets will lower interest rates and stimulate investment, and so partly offset the depressing effect on incomes of the enhanced desire to hold assets. In neither case will this induced change in the pattern of demand prevent the change in incomes altogether, since a change in interest rates cannot prevent the change in incomes that caused it. It may even fail to offset completely the perverse direct effect of the change in incomes on investment, but will probably render it smaller.

Our initial conclusion therefore remains basically unchanged. The main effect of a balanced excess supply of assets is to raise, that of a balanced excess demand to lower incomes. Investment and the supply of assets will be affected only indirectly and so little that even the direction of the change is in doubt, since the changes in income and interest rates pull in opposite directions.

B. CHANGES IN THE SUPPLY OF ASSETS: UNBALANCED EXCESS

While so far we assumed the initial change to be a balanced change, and the initial excess demand or excess supply of assets to be a balanced excess, one may well ask whether this was a realistic assumption to make. The answer to this question clearly depends on what causes the excess. It may be caused by a spontaneous change in the desire to hold or accumulate assets, or by the creation (or destruction) of assets. It seems plausible that the former should lead to a balanced, and the latter to an unbalanced excess of demand or supply. If this is so, it follows that the argument of the last section applies unqualifiedly to changes in the *demand* for holding assets, in the sense that such changes will merely raise or lower incomes but are not likely to affect investment by changing security prices, interest rates, or the banks' ability to lend, except to the limited extent that they change the transactions demand for holding money.

By contrast, changes in the *supply* of a particular type of assets create an unbalanced excess supply or demand, which affects not only incomes but, by changing asset prices, also investment and the accumulation of assets. Moreover, depending on the particular type of assets whose supply is changed, a given impact on incomes may equally well be associated with a similar or with a contrary impact on investment. As an example of each case, we shall discuss an increase, first, in the stock of fixed-interest bearing securities, second, in the supply of cash.

The issue of new fixed-interest bearing securities adds to the net supply of assets if it either adds to the national debt or goes hand-in-hand with investment in real assets. In either case, the deficit spending or the investment has multiplier effects on incomes, additional to those created by the accumulation of assets in people's portfolios. To keep these from complicating the analysis, we shall assume that the issue of fixed-interest bearing securities is either unchanged over time at the rate ΔA, or growing at the same rate, *n,* at which the rest of the economy is growing. In the first case, incomes will rise only because the accumulation of assets in people's portfolios makes them more affluent and more disposed to spend; and the extent of the rise will be shown on p. 52 above. In the second case, an added component is the rise in incomes by $\frac{n}{1-\alpha}\Delta A$, owing to the multiplier effects of the *rise* in deficit spending or investment; and the total rise in incomes therefore will be:

$$\Delta Y = \frac{a_3 - \alpha r + n}{1 - \alpha} \Delta A.$$

The fraction in the above expression is again a multiplier, since it shows the ratio of a rise in incomes to the rise in assets that engendered it. Its reciprocal, which may be called the marginal asset-to-income ratio, is identical with expression (3) of chapter 2, which showed the equilibrium ratio of total assets to total incomes. It appears therefore that when assets accumulate at the long-run growth rate, the marginal asset-to-income ratio and the equilibrium total asset-to-income ratio are equal.

If the accumulation of assets results from deficit spending, the rise in incomes will be a real rise as long as employment can rise. It will only be a nominal rise after full employment or full-capacity production has been reached, since then only prices will rise. On the other hand, if the accumulating assets represent real investment in added capacity or increased productivity, the parallel growth of effective demand and ability to produce can raise incomes not only in a real sense, but in a way that neither leads to a rise in employment nor creates inflationary pressures.

In addition to the rise in incomes engendered by increased spending out of the increased net value of total assets, the creation of fixed-interest bearing assets also raises the proportion they constitute of the total stock of all assets outstanding, thereby lowering their market prices and raising market rates of interest. Furthermore, the rise in incomes raises the transaction demand for holding money, which, in the face of an unchanged supply of money, tends to lower asset prices and raise interest rates yet further.

The fall in the market prices of fixed-interest bearing assets tends to counteract the effect that the increase in their physical quantity has on the net value of all asset holdings, thus slowing the rise in incomes.[3] The rise in interest rates will inhibit the further accumulation of both real capital and financial assets, thus going counter to the stimulating effect of the rise in incomes. If the creation of financial assets is paralleled by the creation of productive real capital, this may, in addition, lower the marginal efficiency of capital and so further discourage the future accumulation of real and financial assets.

The argument would be essentially the same if we had considered instead the accumulation of equities. In this case too, the addition to the stock of assets stimulates spending and so raises incomes, the increased proportion of equities in the total of all assets lowers their prices, raises market rates of interest, and slows the rise in the net value of all assets and with it the rise in incomes. The rise in incomes and the rise in interest rates exert contrary influences on further investment and asset accumulation.

In both cases, the fall in asset prices, the rise in interest rates, and their restraining effect can be offset and nullified by the creation of money. Indeed, the case of financial assets and real capital, productivity and income levels all expanding at the same rate will be recognized as simple secular growth, which calls for a corresponding expansion also of the money supply if growth is to continue.

It will be useful at this stage to make a short digression into the theory of growth. We just mentioned that if the accumulation of assets and of real capital proceed parallel, the one will raise effective demand, the other the

[3]Depending on the price elasticity of demand for holding assets, the fall in the price of assets could offset partly, fully, or more than fully the effect on net value of the increases in quantity. In the absence of empirical information, we tentatively assume elastic demand and partial offsetting, so that net value changes with quantity, though in lesser proportion.

ability to produce; and a parallel rise in both may raise incomes without prices or even employment changing. This is the ideal case. The rise in demand depends on the marginal asset-to-income ratio just discussed, the rise in the ability to produce depends mainly on the incremental capital-output ratio; and it is unlikely that the two should mesh so perfectly as to leave completely unchanged labor-force and capacity utilization. The problems that arise when this is not the case are among the main problems of the theory of growth, more familiar there as the problems created by discrepancies between the warranted and the natural rates of growth.

This is not the place to discuss the theory of growth; but we must at least recall the definition of these two terms, introduced by Harrod.[4] The natural rate has to do with technology and is defined as the rate of capital accumulation that, given the rate of technical progress, would keep the number of potential jobs growing at the same rate at which the labor force is growing. The warranted rate of growth has to do with aggregate effective demand and is defined as the rate of capital accumulation that, given society's propensity to consume, would keep unchanged the percentage of unemployed.

When the warranted rate exceeds the natural rate, as is likely in developed countries, the investment of full-employment savings would be more than enough to provide with equipment accretions to the labor force and the workers freed by the increase in labor productivity.[5] This is the case where the marginal asset-to-income ratio exceeds the incremental capital-output ratio, so that for almost any level of employment and saving, capacity grows faster than effective demand. This would create a secular decline in labor-force and capacity utilization, unless equilibrating forces rectified the situation. In the opposite case, believed typical for developing countries, the natural rate exceeds the warranted rate and the incremental capital-output ratio exceeds the marginal asset-to-income ratio, which is why the creation of additional capacity is accompanied by a *greater* creation of effective demand. This would engender a secular inflationary trend, unless equilibrating forces intervened here too. These are slow, long-run tendencies, overlaid and obscured in the short run by business fluctuations and stabilization policies, but likely to persist until equilibrating forces or corrective policies remove the discrepancy. Changes in interest rates, in technology, and in the ratio of consumer-good to capital-good prices may affect the capital-output ratio; unemployment

[4]Cf. R. F. Harrod, "An Essay in Dynamic Theory", *Economic Journal*, Vol. 49 (1939) pp. 14–33; also his *Towards A Dynamic Economics*, (Macmillan & Co. London, 1948), Lecture Three.

[5]Cf. John M. Power, "Laborsaving and Economic Growth", *American Economic Review, Proceedings*, Vol. 52 (1962) pp. 39–45.

and inflation may influence the public's desired asset-to-income ratio;[6] but all this belongs in the theory of growth, with which we shall no more be concerned. We shall discuss, however, in section C of chapter 8 and section B of chapter 11, the equilibrating influence of international and interregional movements of factors.

We can now proceed to consider our other example of a change in the supply of assets: an excess supply of assets unbalanced in the opposite direction, created by an increase in the supply of cash. Again to make sure that the additional cash represents an addition also to the net value of the total stock of assets, we shall assume that the cash is either printed by Government, or obtained by it against newly issued national debt sold to the central bank, or issued against an inflow of gold from abroad, which finances a payments surplus created by an excess of exports over imports. Cash created in one of these ways may be called outside cash, to distinguish it from inside cash, the creation of which leaves the net supply of all assets unchanged. This will be discussed in the next section.

The creation of outside cash has the same effect on spending and incomes as the creation of any other type of asset. Through its effect on spending, it will raise incomes in approximately the same proportion in which the additional cash stands to the net value of all assets outstanding. Beyond this, it increases the share of cash in the total stock of assets, which will raise the market prices of other assets and lower market rates of interest. The rise in the market prices of other assets makes a further addition to the net value of the stock of assets and so provides a further stimulus to spending and incomes; the lowering of market rates of interest stimulates investment. Here, then, is the case where asset creation, through its impact on spending, asset values and interest rates has mutually *reinforcing* effects on income and activity levels rather than mutually offsetting ones. This is why changes in the supply of money are used as a tool of economic policy.

In the next section, we shall analyze in detail the way in which a change in the supply of cash *in relation to* the supply of other assets affects income and activity levels; let us summarize here the various ways in which an excess supply of assets sets into motion forces that

[6]Cf. James Tobin, "Money and Economic Growth", *Econometrica,* Vol. 33 (1965) pp. 671–84, for the monetary side of such adjustment.

restore equilibrium. We saw that a balanced excess supply affects primarily the demand for holding assets by raising, through the Pigou effect, the level of income. An unbalanced excess supply will, in addition, have a primary effect also on the supply of assets. An excess supply of interest- or dividend-bearing assets will lower the value of outstanding assets and, by raising interest rates, restrict investment and slow the creation of new assets; an excess supply of cash will raise asset values and, by lowering interest rates, stimulate investment and new asset creation. In the former case, the demand for assets expands and their supply diminishes to restore equilibrium between the two; in the latter, demand and supply both expand and the supply expansion restores to equilibrium merely the *share* of different types of assets in their total supply. It is obvious that equilibrium in this last case is restored at a higher asset supply and with a higher level of income than in the two other cases.

C. EXCESS SUPPLY OF LIQUIDITY

Earlier sections of this chapter were concerned with discrepancies between the total supply of assets and the total demand for them, accompanied or unaccompanied by discrepancies between the pattern of demand and the pattern of supply. This section will concentrate on discrepancies between, and changes in, the pattern of supply and the pattern of demand for assets, while initially the net value of all assets remains unchanged and equal to the demand for holding them. Our example of such discrepancies will be an excess supply of liquidity, brought about by the creation of cash *and a simultaneous reduction* in the supply of other assets.

When the central bank buys securities in the open market, it puts cash into circulation equal in value to the securities it withdraws from circulation. Such open market operations therefore leave unchanged the physical volume of assets in the public's hands and merely increase the proportion that cash in circulation forms of an unchanged total of asset holdings. Hence the name "inside cash" for cash so created. But the central bank's purchase of other assets is likely to bid up their prices, which will not only lower interest rates but also increase the net value of the public's total asset holdings as well as its spending out of assets, though probably less than if outside cash had been created. The main influence, however, of inside cash creation is exerted through interest rates and its impact on commercial banks and their policies. Interest rates are lowered not only directly, through the central bank's bidding up of asset prices, but also indirectly, through pressure on the commercial banks to do the same. For much of the cash injected into the economy is bound to find its way to the commercial banks, add to their excess reserves, and so induce them to bid up security prices further or otherwise ease the terms of lending. In the United States, the commercial banks hold about 40 per cent of all cash (together with saving institutions they hold almost one half); and they are likely to obtain a similar proportion also of marginal additions to the supply of cash. The importance of this lies in the fact that the banks, unlike the general public, are not content to change the ratio of their cash to other asset holdings in response to changes in interest rates. They try, mostly with success, to keep this ratio close to the minimum reserve ratio prescribed by the monetary authority.

Over the past 20 years, the U.S. commercial banks' excess reserves (i.e., reserves over the legally required minimum) averaged 1.3 per cent of required reserves and fluctuated around this average with a standard deviation of only 1.7 per cent. Only during the exceptional periods of the war and the great depression did their reserves exceed the legal minimum by a substantial amount.

As soon, therefore, as the central bank creates cash by buying securities, the commercial banks find themselves with more excess reserves and are prompted to create deposit money either by buying securities or by extending loans to customers, either of which will lower interest rates further. The credit multiplier, discussed in section B of chapter 3, shows the leverage this gives to the central bank in prompting the creation of money through its creation of cash.

Our main interest at this stage, however, lies not in the amount of money created but in the stimulating impact of the creation of cash on investment and the economy. This depends very much on whether the commercial banks create deposits by buying securities or by making loans to customers.

When commercial banks buy securities, they create *inside* deposit money in exactly the same way in which the central bank's open-market buying of securities creates *inside* cash. They increase the quantity of money and its share in the public's total asset holdings but leave unchanged the volume of primary securities and raise the net value of all assets only to the extent that they bid up security prices.

Very different is the creation of deposits through the extension of loans to customers. When a bank makes a loan to a customer, a primary financial asset is created; and the customer, unless he is a speculator, creates real assets with the proceeds. In short, the money commercial banks create by extending loans to customers is usually *outside* deposit money, because it coincides with an increase in primary securities and real assets.

To gauge the share of this in the total money created, we recall that loans to customers constitute around two thirds of the portfolio of U.S. commercial banks. This means that if the central bank buys $1 billion worth of securities, it will, in the long run, cause the commercial banks to add $1.8 billion to their portfolios,[7] of which as much as $1.2 billion may be the increase in loans to customers. In other words, the creation of inside cash at the rate of $1 billion may directly add $1.2 billion to the level of investment for as long a period as the creation of cash continues. In addition, the purchase of securities from the public by the central and commercial banks at an annual rate of $1.6 billion[8] is almost certain to raise security prices and lower interest rates, thus stimulating investment yet further. Finally, the faster accumulation of assets resulting from the higher level of investment also stimulates, through its wealth effect, consumer spending.

Before we qualify this rather too definite and formal statement, it may be worth contrasting it to the effects of the creation of outside cash. What would happen if a $1 billion annual export surplus led to an annual inflow of $1 billion of gold, which prompted the commercial banks to create deposits by an annual $1.8 billion expansion of their loans and portfolios? The level of investment would now be $2.2 billion higher, since to the $1.2 billion annual investment out of loans by the banks' customers we must now add the $1 billion foreign investment that the export surplus represents; and the wealth effect of asset accumulation on consumer spending would also be correspond-

[7]In view of the 2.8 value of the credit multiplier. See p. 33 above.

[8]$1 billion by the central bank and $.6 billion ($1.8 b – $1.2 b) by the commercial banks.

ingly greater. At the same time, with the banks' purchase of securities from the public proceeding at a slower rate, (being now confined to the commercial banks' annual purchase of $0.6 billion) security prices would be raised and interest rates lowered to a lesser extent.

To summarize, whether the newly created cash is inside or outside cash, the total amount of money created will be the same and generally contain both inside and outside money, though naturally more inside money in the first than in the second case. Increases in outside money are linked with equal additions to investment;[9] and they also stimulate investment indirectly by lowering interest rates. Inside money provides only an indirect stimulus to investment by lowering interest rates but is likely to lower them more than outside money does. Both of them raise the value of the public's asset holdings and with it consumer spending out of assets, but outside money probably more so, because it raises the net value of assets not only by raising their prices but by adding to their volume outstanding as well.

An important distinction between the direct provision of investment on the one hand and the indirect stimulation of investment and consumer spending on the other is that the former is proportional to the *rate* at which money is created; whereas the latter grows with the *stock* of money or assets created. This probably means that in the short run at least, outside money creation is the more effective in stimulating the economy; but empirical evidence on the relative effectiveness of the two types of money creation is still lacking.

The argument so far was based on the assumption that commercial banks apportion marginal additions to their reserves between loans and investments in the same ratio in which their total loans and investments stand to each other in their balance sheet. This is not always so. For banks to be able to extend loans to customers, they

[9]To see why an increase in outside money usually coincides with investment in the same amount, one must consider the different ways of putting additional money into circulation. This can be done by giving people money: i) in exchange for other assets, ii) in exchange for currently produced goods, iii) as a loan to enable them to buy goods, iv) as a gift. The first creates inside money, the others create outside money. The goods relinquished against or bought with the outside money represent investment—at least in the sense of having the same multiplier effects on income as investment. When the newly created money is put into circulation as a gift, we have outside money with no corresponding investment; this, being a rare and unlikely case, was ignored in the above analysis.

need customers willing to borrow; and these are not always there. The supply of securities available to banks is bound always to be more elastic than the supply of customers willing to borrow; there may also be times when securities are more profitable to hold than loans. The so-called liquidity trap is an example. When market-rates of interest are low, and the belief that they have reached their limit is universally and firmly held, monetary policy may be powerless to stimulate the economy. The central bank's open-market purchase of securities will fail to raise their prices and lower interest rates; similarly, the commercial banks' purchase of securities will also leave security prices unchanged; and if they do not or cannot extend loans at the same time, all the money created will be inside money, and interest rates, investment and the level of activity will all be unchanged.

This is likely to happen only when the cash created is inside cash, which does not directly raise investment. By contrast, the additional investment that goes hand-in-hand with an increase in outside cash is likely, through its multiplied effect on incomes, to increase the public's demand for bank loans at the very time when their increased reserves enable the commercial banks to extend such loans. An increase in outside cash therefore has a better chance of leading to outside and inside deposit-creation in the proportions suggested above. This means that in their ability to stimulate the economy, the difference between an increase in inside and in outside cash may well be very much greater than appears from the formal analysis of these differences.

D. EXCESS DEMAND FOR LIQUIDITY

Our discussion in the previous section of the economic consequences of the creation of cash applies *pari passu* also to the symmetrical case of the destruction of cash—up to a point. It will have all the parallel restraining effects on the economy. The reduced share of money in total assets will raise interest rates; the destruction of outside money will lower investment, and indirectly, through the Pigou effect, restrain consumer spending. But the destruction of cash, or failure to create cash in step with the increased demand for holding it, may have another effect as well: it may lead to the development of new forms of liquidity or new ways of economizing on the use of money.

It was assumed so far that the supply of money is determined by the deliberate policy of the monetary authority, not by the automatic forces of the market. This is correct to the extent that the quantity of cash is fully determined by the monetary authority and that the quantity of deposit money and near moneys is fully determined by the quantity of cash—at least as long as the public persists in its established habits of using the various forms of money and near money. There is evidence, however, that when restrictive monetary policy leads to a great rise in interest rates, the public may develop new means of economizing in the use of money and financial intermediaries may develop new indirect securities, which the public may adopt as new forms of money or new substitutes for it. An important characteristic of such changes is that they are often irreversible.

Little can be said about the public's economizing the use of money. Money offers a convenience, part of which may be relinquished if the reward for relinquishing it (interest) is high. Many firms have learned to keep some of their liquid assets on savings accounts, in short-term securities and in Certificates of Deposit; and once they have established such a routine, it remains the routine.

More interesting is the development of new forms of money or near money. Since the price of money, in terms of money, is unchangeable, this does not happen by excess demand driving up the price and so increasing the profitability of supplying money. It happens instead by high interest rates rendering lending more profitable and so encouraging would-be lenders to seek new ways of obtaining the funds to lend out. The way to obtain funds is to sell assets more attractive or more convenient than those already available; and if the public buys them, they become new forms of money or quasi money. For example, savings deposits in the United States have increased from equal to almost double the supply of money over a 7-year period. This clearly shows a great change either in the public's asset-holding habits or in the attractiveness of savings deposits. In either case, this great addition to the supply of liquidity was brought about largely by the savings and loan associations, over whose liquidity creation the monetary authority has no control, and its was probably sparked or greatly encouraged by the monetary authority's restictive and high interest-rate policies.

Bibliography to Chapter 5

Most of this chapter is a restatement in the language of Modigliani's asset theory of the theory of the multiplier as contained in Keynes' *General Theory of Employment, Interest and Money*. For the concepts and distinction between inside and outside money, see Lloyd A. Metzler, "Wealth, Saving, and the Rate of Interest," *Journal of Political Economy*, Vol. 59 (1951) pp. 93–116.

Chapter 6

Money and the price level

The first use, perhaps, to which economists have put their analysis of the supply of and demand for money was to explain the price level, and variations in the price level. In an early version of the quantity theory of money, David Hume likened money to a liquid poured into a vessel and identified the level of this liquid with the price level. This is still the picture that first comes to many people's minds when the subject is mentioned; and it is not a bad picture for visualizing what happens in hyperinflations. A recent statistical study of the seven hyperinflations of history has shown that in their case, the quantity theory of money is a reasonable first approximation to reality.[1]

In less extreme cases, however, and especially in today's complex economy, the causal chain through which a change in the supply of money influences the price level is long and tenuous; and economists no longer believe in a relation as simple, mechanical, and invariable as Hume's simile would suggest. As a matter of fact, most modern theories of inflation go to the opposite extreme and bypass the theory

[1]Cf. Philip Cagan, "The Monetary Dynamics of Hyperinflation," in Milton Friedman, ed., *Studies in the Quantity Theory of Money*, (Chicago, 1956) Chapter 2.

of money completely, neglecting altogether the influence of changes in the stock of money. They try instead to explain the price level as a function of such real variables as aggregate effective demand and cost conditions that determine product prices, and the institutional and other factors that influence the wage contract negotiated between management and organized labor. All these are factors outside the scope of this book; but we must deal with the influence, if any, of the stock of money on aggregate effective demand and thereby on the price level.

The obvious and simple way of doing this is to ask, and try to answer, two questions. The first is whether the monetary authority's refusal to increase the stock of money could effectively keep prices from rising, at a time when real factors, such as those just mentioned, would call for a rise. The second question is whether the monetary authority can always increase the stock of money, and thereby raise effective demand and ultimately the price level, even at a time when other influences pull in the opposite direction.

The orthodox answer to the first question used to run as follows. Money is essential for carrying out the many transactions of a monetary economy; and when prices rise, the value of these transactions, and with it the need for money, rises in proportion.[2] The monetary authority, however, can prevent the rise in prices by refusing to increase the supply of money. For, when prices and the value of transactions rise, people are inconvenienced by an unchanged supply of money and will try to escape the inconvenience by building up their supplies of it. Each person's attempt to do so, however, reduces his expenditures and so contributes to creating a deflationary or anti-inflationary force that will prevent the rise in prices. While the public cannot add to the stock of money in circulation and so restore its previous ratio to the flow of transactions, each person's attempt to add to his money holdings cuts the flow of transactions and helps in that way to restore the previous ratio.

The argument is convincing when applied to a primitive economy, in which money is the main financial asset and the main means of

[2]Contrary to appearances, this does *not* contradict the argument of chapter 4, according to which the transactions demand for money rises with the square root of the volume of transactions, because that argument was based on the assumption of unchanged prices and a rise in the *real* volume of transactions.

storing general purchasing power. A person short of money and wanting to replenish his stock of it has no alternative in such an economy but to cut the flow of his expenditures, so restricting output and restraining the rise in prices. In such an economy therefore, a refusal to increase the supply of money is very likely to be effective in preventing a rise in prices.[3]

By contrast, in a complex economy, where money is just one of many kinds of financial assets and represents a small fraction of the total stock of wealth, the above argument does not ring true. Insufficient holdings of money in such an economy prompt, not a cut in expenditure flows, but a desire to replenish money holdings through the sale of other assets; leading, not to a reduction in output, but to a fall in asset prices and rise in yields. These changes can and often do inhibit consumer spending and business investment, thus reducing the flow of output; but the way in which they do this is not so simple and direct, nor so mechanically determined as the quantity theory of money would have it. As a result, the extent to which they reduce output is quite variable, depending on the response of spending and investment to changes in asset prices and yields, and on the response of these to the change in the demand for holding money.

The fall in the prices and rise in the yields of assets discourage their sale and must proceed to the point where they prevent it and persuade the public to make do with its unchanged stock of money. How soon this point is reached depends very much on the complexity and sophistication of the financial system. The larger the number of near-monies and money substitutes in the system, and the greater their elasticity of substitution for money, the smaller the change in asset prices and yields necessary to make the public live with its unchanged stock of money. In addition, an incipient rise in yields can greatly stimulate the ingenuity of financial intermediaries in developing new debt instruments and of the public in devising new

[3]An alternative way of presenting the same argument is the following. Throughout much of this book, we stressed the influence of asset holdings on spending (aggregate effective demand). This could be called the quantity theory of assets, since it attributes to assets much the same influence that the quantity theorists used to attribute to money. In a simple economy therefore, with a primitive financial structure, and where money is the main form of asset, our quantity theory of assets becomes indistinguishable from the old-fashioned quantity theory of money.

uses for old debt instruments, thus helping to overcome a shortage of money without an increase in its supply, without too much change in asset prices and yields, and without much of a restraining effect therefore on incomes, employment and prices.

Indeed, the present complexity of our financial system, the many forms of money and near money now in circulation, are living testimony to past ingenuity in developing new forms of money in response to the failure of the supply of old forms of money to keep up with the demand. This was discussed briefly at the end of chapter 5 and is recalled here as a factor that limits the monetary authority's restrictive power.

At the same time, however, the complexity and flexibility of the financial system and the limits its flexibility set to the monetary authority's powers of control, hinge on there being a fair degree of price stability. The entire superstructure of moneys, near moneys and money substitutes built on cash in our financial system consists of debt instruments that promise future payment in terms of cash. Not only does the real value of the stock of such debt instruments decline absolutely and relatively to other assets in periods of inflation; but it also becomes very difficult to replenish the declining real stock of these debt instruments if past inflation leads to the expectation of its future continuance. The public will accept and use near moneys and money substitutes in lieu of money only as long as it has faith in their undiminished future value. Expected inflation destroys this faith and with it the demand for debt instruments based on it.

It is true that the expectation of rising prices reduces the attractiveness not only of near moneys and money substitutes but of money proper as well. Its advantage, however, of being general purchasing power in one's pocket, universally acceptable and immediately spendable, is so great that people continue to hold money even when they fully expect it to depreciate in their pockets. They will hold less money at such times and economize on its use; but since this enhances the premium on immediate spendability, it is also likely to enhance the superiority of immediately spendable money proper, over not-so-immediately spendable money substitutes. In short, when the expectation of rising prices causes people to cut down on their holdings of liquid reserves, they will sooner cut down on their bank deposits and savings deposits than on the cash they carry in their pockets. This is why prolonged inflation and the expectation of future inflation tend to keep the financial system in a primitive stage, or make it revert to such a stage.

We can now proceed to our second question, whether the monetary authorities can always increase the supply of money and thereby raise effective demand. Most of the answer to this question was contained in section C of chapter 5. We argued there that the creation of inside money never, while that of outside money usually, goes hand-in-hand with investment; and therefore with the creation of effective demand and its stimulating multiplier effects on income. In addition, of course, the creation of both kinds of money tends to ease the terms of credit, which will indirectly stimulate investment and effective demand, provided conditions are otherwise favorable for the public to make use of the easier terms of credit. We also argued that the creation of outside cash was an excellent way of making the public receptive to the banks' easing the terms of credit.

The answer is contained here; and it is clearly a no. While the monetary authority can always increase the quantity of cash in circulation, unaided it can create only inside cash. The additional cash will always prompt the commercial banks to create additional deposit money; but under unfavorable conditions they too can create only inside deposit money; and effective demand in such circumstances is unlikely to be raised at all. In short, inside money creation may be completely ineffective as a stimulant of economic activity; and inside money is all that monetary policy can create if conditions are unfavorable. Deficit spending by Government or by the outside world (i.e., an excess of exports over imports) is needed to turn inside into outside cash; and this is also one of the more effective ways of creating the favorable conditions that render the public receptive to easier bank terms and lower interest rates. In short, merely to create money is not enough— it also has to be spent (i.e., effective demand must also be created) if the level of economic activity is to be raised.

Bibliography to Chapter 6

Very little that is worth reading has been written in recent years about the influence of monetary factors on prices and the rate of price increase;

more sadly lacking still are good discussions of the relation between monetary and real factors as causes of inflation. On the latter subject, however, see Harry G. Johnson, "A Survey of Theories of Inflation," *The Indian Economic Review*, Vol. 6 (1963) pp. 29–66; on the former, see A. J. Brown, *The Great Inflation, 1939–51* (London, 1955), Philip Cagan, "The Monetary Dynamics of Hyperinflation," and Milton Friedman, "The Quantity Theory of Money—A Restatement," these last two in M. Friedman (ed.), *Studies in the Quantity Theory of Money*, (Chicago, 1956). On the general subject of inflation, see also Charles L. Schultze, *Recent Inflation in the United States*, Study Paper N°1, U.S. Congress, Joint Economic Committee, *Studies of Employment, Growth and Price Levels*, (Gov. Printing Office, Washington, 1959); and C. Bresciani-Turroni, *The Economics of Inflation* (Allen & Unwin, London, 1937). The last-mentioned is a classic, still well worth reading both for its excellent analysis of the German hyperinflation of 1923 and for its account of the often absurd theoretical explanations current not so long ago.

Part B

The Balance of Payments

Chapter 7

The national and international accounts

We begin with a discussion of the national and international accounts and their relation, because this seems the best introduction to the subject of balance-of-payments adjustment and balance-of-payments problems. To understand the national income accounts of a closed economy, one must start with the Keynesian identity between total receipts and total payments. The flow of total receipts equals the flow of total payments, because they are the same transactions looked at from different people's points of view. One person's payments are necessarily some other person's (or persons') receipts; and when all the people who make payments and all those who receive them belong to the same closed economy, the sum total of everybody's payments must necessarily equal the sum total of everybody's receipts.

The sum total of all payments and of all receipts, however, are amorphous and meaningless aggregates, made up of too many different kinds of transactions. They can be reduced to the more meaningful aggregates of total expenditure on final goods and total receipts of income for services rendered, by omitting items that are irrelevant or involve double counting. In particular, one must subtract from total payments and receipts those connected with the transfer from one person's ownership to another's of assets already in existence; one must also subtract the transfer of part of a person's income to another, made not in payment for services rendered (in which case it would be additional income), but merely to let him share in the fun or burden of spending it. Finally, to avoid double counting, transactions involving intermediate goods must also be subtracted, since their value is included in that of the final goods they enter. There remain, on the one side, payments for final goods and services, on the other, receipts of income for services rendered; and these are again identically equal, because each of the transfers and intermediate transactions subtracted involved both a payment and a receipt and so represented equal deductions from the payments and receipts sides. In a closed economy therefore one can deduce the equality of total expenditure on final output with total incomes earned from the identity of total payments and total receipts.

In the open economy, the total receipts of residents cease to equal the total payments of residents. The people who make the payments and those who receive them often do, but sometimes do not, belong to the same economy, which is why total receipts and total payments tend to move together but are not necessarily equal. This state of affairs, the tendency of receipts and payments to move in the same direction but without a tendency to equality, will be the subject matter of chapter 8. Here, we shall explore some of the formal relations between these magnitudes.

A. THE RELATION BETWEEN THE NATIONAL AND THE INTERNATIONAL ACCOUNTS

If we divide residents' total receipts, R, and residents' total payments, P, into their domestic and foreign components according to the domicile of the other party to the transaction; and if we remember the argument of the previous paragraphs, then it appears that domestic receipts and domestic payments must be identically equal, so that the following relation holds:

$$R - P = (R_d + R_f) - (P_d + P_f) = R_f - P_f = B,$$

where B denotes the balance of international payments. In the open economy, total receipts may differ from total payments, and their difference equals the difference between *foreign* receipts and *foreign* payments, also known as the country's net balance of international payments.

We may again proceed from global aggregate receipts and payments to receipts of income and expenditure on final goods. If we divide asset transfers, income transfers, and transactions in intermediate goods, into their domestic and foreign components, and recall that receipts and payments are identically equal for each domestic transaction, then the domestic components of all these can be subtracted from both aggregate receipts and aggregate payments without changing the equality. The retention of foreign receipts and payments for intermediate goods, and their bracketing with foreign receipts and payments for all other goods, is as it should be; because, from the country's own point of view, intermediate goods exported become final goods, intermediate goods imported become primary resources, and their inclusion in the national accounts involves no double counting. If then, we ignore for the moment foreign transfers of income as unimportant, we find that a country's net balance of international payments is identically equal with the sum of the net balance between its income receipts and final expenditures and the net balance of its external transfers of assets.

The meaning of this identity is best seen if for a moment one assumes a zero net balance, first in the transfer of assets, and then between incomes and expenditures. When net asset transfers are nil, a country's balance of payments will be favorable or unfavorable, depending on whether its inhabitants earn more than they spend or spend more than they earn. This equality is often cited by those who, to stress their disapprobation of an unfavorable balance of payments, equate this to the profligate habit of spending in excess of earnings. But this equality holds only in the special case when net asset transfers are nil. When one assumes instead equality between income earnings and final expenditures, then the net balance of international payments becomes equal to the balance between asset inflows and asset outflows. In other words, keeping expenditures within earnings is no guaranty against an unfavorable balance of payments, which will still arise if imported assets exceed in value those exported.

It is worth considering in this connection the meaning of asset transfers. In the domestic realm, asset transfers are considered so uninteresting and unimportant that we do not even collect statistics. After all, they change not the distribution of wealth but merely the form in which different people hold wealth. In international relations, the same asset transfers can be a major cause of payments disturbances. In particular, people's desire to exchange domestic for foreign assets in their portfolios will create an unfavorable balance of payments even if current spending stays within current earnings.

The components of the balance of payments, as listed in official statistics, need not be discussed here in detail; but it may be useful to distinguish those that link the different concepts used in the national accounts and so bring into focus the relation between these and the international accounts. Starting out from *national expenditure,* one subtracts imports and adds exports of final goods and services in order to obtain the *domestic product.* In other words, the difference between domestic product and national expenditure equals the balance of trade—if this is defined as exports minus imports of not only goods but also final services.

Thanks to the Keynesian identity between payments and receipts, the value of the domestic product equals the *national income generated* inside the country; but to this one must add foreign incomes earned by people at home and subtract domestic incomes accruing to people abroad in order to obtain *national income earned.* Since incomes are payments and receipts for productive services rendered, the difference between national income earned and national expenditure equals the balance of trade in goods and services—with services this time including not only final but also productive services. If next, national income earned is augmented by transfer incomes from abroad and diminished by incomes transferred to abroad, one obtains *national income available* within the country. The difference between national income available and national expenditure equals the balance of payments on current account:

$$Y - E = T_d.$$

For some purposes it is useful to express this last equality in slightly different form. Writing national income available as the sum of consumption and saving ($Y = C + S$), national expenditure as the sum of consumption and investment ($E = C + I$), and the current account of the balance of payments as the difference between exports and imports broadly interpreted ($T_d = X - M$), the above equality becomes

$$S - I = X - M$$

or

$$S + M = I + X.$$

What used to be the equality of saving and investment in the closed economy becomes, in the open economy, the equality of the difference between saving and investment and the difference between exports and imports, or the equality between the sum of savings and imports and the sum of investment and exports. Just as in the closed economy, these equalities can be interpreted either as identities between statistically ascertainable ex-post quantities, or as equilibrium conditions between quantities interpreted in the ex-ante sense as planned or intended magnitudes.

B. THE BALANCE OF PAYMENTS

Since we do not regard as money the foreign currencies foreigners use for this purpose; and our currency is not money from their point of view, virtually every international transaction is barter for one of the parties concerned. The significance of barter is its equivalence to two monetary transactions: a sale and a purchase. If an American producer sells shirts to Brazil for cruseiros, he is engaging in barter: a sale of shirts and a purchase of what we shall call short-term claims on Brazil. If he sells the shirts for U.S. dollars, then it is the Brazilian importer who engages in barter; a purchase of shirts and a sale of short-term claims on the United States. Sometimes a person engages in barter of this type because he has simultaneously made the two separate decisions to buy the one commodity and sell the other. Mostly, however, people barter not because they want to but because it is unavoidable in international transactions and because they can engage in a complementary transaction, which, combined with the barter, turns this into a single monetary transaction. The American who sells shirts for cruseiros usually does so because he can sell these for dollars; and the Brazilian who buys shirts for dollars does it because he can buy the dollars for cruseiros. Virtually every international transaction is matched by a complementary transaction in the foreign exchange market where one currency is sold for another. For a study therefore of equilibrium and disequilibrium in the balance of payments, one may just as well concentrate on the market for foreign exchange.

If this were like a commodity market, where supply and demand are equated by price adjustment, we would have flexible exchange rates and no balance-of-payments problems. The foreign exchange market, however, does not operate this way; and we do not even know if it could, because it never has. An isolated country has occasionally had flexible exchange rates in a world where all other countries kept their exchanges fixed; but one cannot generalize from its experience to how a system of universally flexible exchange rates would operate. This remains therefore an untried experiment, advocated by a small but increasing number of professional economists and abhorred by most businessmen and bankers, who believe that the uncertainty flexible rates would bring to economic life would be too high a price to pay for the solution of balance-of-payments problems.

In most foreign-exchange markets, prices are stabilized. Today, most countries' monetary authorities are pledged by international agreement (as signatories of the charter of the International Monetary Fund) to maintain the value of their currency in terms of foreign currencies within margins of one per cent on each side of parity. In the past, their pledge to buy and sell gold at a fixed price against domestic currency accomplished very much the same thing. In either case, price is kept stable by *accommodating* purchases and sales of gold and/or foreign currency, which are additional to the *autonomous* purchases and sales of gold and foreign currency by those who need or obtain it in the course of ordinary foreign transactions they engage in for profit.

Accommodating transactions are carried out first of all by the monetary authority, whose task it is to keep exchange rates stable, and which keeps a reserve of gold and/or foreign currencies with which to accomplish this. Moreover, once the monetary authority is committed, and known to be committed to keep exchange rates stable, others too may engage in accommodating transactions and hold reserves with which to do so. For example, commercial banks may, to accommodate their customers, hold foreign currency reserves and be willing to add to or draw down these reserves. Such changes in their reserves will be accommodating not only to their customers but also in the sense of helping to maintain exchange rates stable.

We can now define equilibrium in the balance of international payments as the equality between the *autonomous* supply of foreign currency and the *autonomous* demand for foreign currency. This is an equilibrium situation, whether there is a monetary authority pledged to keep exchange rates stable but not having to interfere to to achieve this, or whether exchange rates are flexible and their movement assures the equality. On this definition therefore, payments disequilibrium is the difference between autonomous supply and autonomous demand; and this can only come about if monetary authority offsets the difference with accommodating transactions, either to keep exchange rates stable or at least to keep them from moving as much as they would otherwise.

The disequilibrium is said to be favorable and the balance of payments in surplus when this difference is positive; the disequilibrium is unfavorable and the payments balance in deficit when the difference is negative. Since the foreign-exchange market is always cleared, the difference between autonomous supply and demand must always be matched by an equal difference between accommodating demand and supply. The extent of payments disequilibrium, therefore, is equally well measured by the net balance of autonomous as by the net balance of accommodating transactions. The difficulty lies in distinguishing the accommodating from the autonomous transactions.

This difficulty stems from the fact that transactions are not tagged as autonomous or accommodating. The intention behind them must be inferred from the identity of the parties and the nature of the transaction. On a narrow definition of accommodating transactions, one would regard as such only official transactions (i.e., where at least one of the parties is a central bank or treasury) and consider all other transactions autonomous. Payments disequilibrium would then be the difference between foreign receipts and foreign payments on all transactions between private parties, equal also to the difference between accommodating payments and receipts on foreign transactions to which central banks and treasuries are parties.

When one tries to broaden the definition in order to include the accommodating transactions of commercial banks, one encounters the problem that not all the foreign short-term claims of commercial banks are held merely to accommodate their customers. Banks hold a portfolio of assets in order to earn interest; and their purchases and sales of foreign short-term claims may be motivated as much by this as by their desire to accommodate customers. How can changes in such holdings be separated into autonomous and accommodating? A rough way to do so is to distinguish between currencies that are and those that are not customarily held as international reserves and to assume that foreign sales and purchases of the former (but not of the latter) are accommodating transactions. This is the distinction used as the basis of the definition of the U.S. balance of payments in U.S. official statistics.

Such difficulties of distinguishing the two types of transactions are avoided by yet another definition of equilibrium, which draws the dividing line between current-account transactions and long-term capital flows on the one hand, and gold and all short-term capital flows on the other. These latter may be called temporary transactions, the former persistent transactions—persistent in the sense that they represent flows that can persist unchanged for a long time. The difference between receipts and payments on persistent transactions has been called basic balance. Equality between payments and receipts on each side of such a dividing line means equilibrium in the basic balance—a situation tenable and satisfactory in the long run. If this coincides with a payments deficit, because an outflow of short-term capital needs to be financed by a sale of gold, payments difficulties can arise only in the short run, since an outflow of short-term capital cannot continue for long. Also, when an outflow of short-term capital is the sole cause of payments deficit, it is easily remedied without much disturbance to the rest of the economy.[1]

Carrying this approach a step further, it has also been argued that the dividing line ought to be drawn between the current account of the balance of payments on the one hand and all other foreign transactions on the other, because only equilibrium on the current account of the payments balance can be considered real long-run equilibrium and maintained indefinitely.

To examine the soundness of this argument, one must investigate the significance of equilibrium in the balance of payments. Equilibrium between autonomous payments and autonomous receipts means a situation in which the stock of a country's external reserves remains unchanged, because they are not needed and not used to stabilize the value of its currency. Equilibrium in the basic balance is a situation in which a country's short-term asset position remains unchanged, whether these are official or privately held, consist of gold, currency, or short-term securities, and where short-term asset position means

[1]Cf. Hal B. Lary, *Problems of the United States as World Trader and Banker* (Princeton: National Bureau of Economic Research, 1963); Walter S. Salant, Emile Despres, Lawrence D. Krause, Alice M. Rivlin, William A. Salant & Lorie Tarshis, *The United States Balance of Payments in 1968* (Washington: The Brookings Institution, 1963).

the difference between the stock of domestically-held foreign, and foreign-held domestic assets. Finally, equilibrium on the current account of the payments balance is a situation in which a country's short- *and* long-term asset position remains unchanged over time.

The significance of the first of these is simple and obvious. Under a regime of fixed exchange rates, the authorities are pledged to intervene if necessary to maintain exchange rates; and equilibrium on the first definition means that, such intervention being unnecessary, the ability to intervene and the resources needed for intervention remain unchanged and unimpaired. Equilibrium on the second definition means an unchanged sum of official reserves *and* net private short-term holdings. This implies that the resources available for future intervention in the foreign-exchange market remain unimpaired if one assumes that private short-term holdings can easily be either induced by interest-rate policy to move in an equilibrating fashion, or appropriated for official use. Equilibrium on the third definition means no change in the country's overall asset position in relation to the outside world. Even if reserves should be depleted and the country's *liquidity* impaired, its *solvency* is unaffected, because the change in reserves is counterbalanced by a contrary change in private asset holdings.

C. THE SOURCES OF DISEQUILIBRIUM

Having defined equilibrium and disequilibrium in the balance of payments, it seems appropriate to deal also with the sources of disequilibrium and distinguish them according to their impact on the domestic economy. This yields a three-fold classification: (i) sources of disequilibrium that simultaneously worsen the balance of payments and lower incomes or improve payments and raise incomes; (ii) those that worsen payments while raising incomes or improve payments while depressing the domestic income level; (iii) finally those that have no impact on incomes.

(i) The first group comprises the classic case of balance-of-payments disturbance, a shift in demand from one country's output to another's, since it is such shifts that cause similar changes in a country's balance of payments and level of income. International capital transfers cause similar disturbances, whether they are occasioned by political exaction, foreign aid, or foreign lending. Most of our attention will be centered on this case, which has received the most attention in the literature and is also the one the most easily managed.

(ii) The second group comprises payments disturbances caused by differences between different countries' cost levels or rates of general price increase. This is the opposite case of the relatively easily managed case of the previous group; and indeed it happens to be the most intractable cause of balance-of-payments disequilibrium.

(iii) Into the third group belong payments disturbances that leave a country's current account unchanged and affect only its liquidity position. They have their source therefore in someone's wish to change the composition of his portfolio of assets. An American's desire to add to his holdings of foreign assets and benefit by their higher yield is one example; a foreigner's desire to obtain long-term loans on the cheaper terms of this country is another; and a third example is that where foreigners, simultaneously with borrowing in this country on long term, lend on short term by buying U.S. short-term securities of the kind used as external reserves. None of these disturbs current-account equilibrium; all of them affect external reserves, and, in the opposite direction, also the country's long-term foreign asset position. The last example is a case where people change their liquidity position; and it is natural to find the country's liquidity position changed accordingly (though in this example, of course, in the opposite direction). The first example, however, need involve no change in the person's liquidity position, yet it affects the country's. The American who buys foreign assets may do so for money obtained by selling domestic assets; but this transaction will nevertheless cause an outflow of U.S. external reserves to pay for the inflow of foreign assets.

After a general discussion of automatic payments adjustment in chapter 8, chapters 9, 10 and 11 will deal with the particular problems and characteristics of each of these groups.

Bibliography to Chapter 7

The *Survey of Current Business* publishes regularly the U.S. official statistics of the national accounts, the balance of international payments, as well as of the stock of foreign investments. For the formal relations between the various aggregate quantities, see Harry G. Johnson, "Towards a General Theory of the Balance of Payments" in his *International Trade and Economic Growth* (Allen & Unwin, 1958).

Chapter 8

The problem of the balance of payments

The last chapter dealt with various concepts and definitions relevant to the balance of international payments of a country. The balance-of-payments concept, however, is much more general. Any group of people and firms (and Governments) has a balance of payments and can have a balance-of-payments problem, whether it consists of a geographical region that is part of a country, or one that comprises several countries, or whether it is defined in some other way, for example, as all the customers of a bank. And for a proper understanding of the balance-of-payments problem of a group, however defined, one must relate it to the balance-of-payments problem or its equivalent of the individual.

A household or firm has current receipts, makes current payments, and may be said to be in current-account equilibrium when the two are equal. When the two are not equal and current receipts exceed current payments, it will accumulate assets; when current payments exceed current receipts, it will draw down previously accumulated assets—unless it can supplement its assets by borrowing and so can either prevent the exhaustion of its accumulated reserves or continue to make losses or spend more than it earns even after their exhaustion. Most people and firms can be trusted to husband their financial resources and to adjust their payments to their receipts or their receipts to their payments whenever they have exhausted, or are unwilling to draw down further, their accumulation of assets or their credit.

But if individual persons and firms can maintain their own current-account equilibrium and depart from it only to the extent and for the duration that their reserves and credit allow, why should a country or other entity consisting of a group of such persons and firms have difficulties in accomplishing the same thing? To answer this question must be the first step in our analysis of the balance-of-payments problem.

Imagine a closed system, such as the world or a self-contained, self-sufficient country, where, as we know, the sum total of receipts of income necessarily equals the sum total of expenditures on final goods. Assume further that the inhabitants hold money and a variety of other assets in quantities they consider appropriate to their incomes. While incomes and expenditures are equal for this world or country taken as a whole, they are not generally equal for each individual member. We can divide these members therefore into two groups such that members of one, taken all together, spend more, and members of the other, all together, spend less, than they earn. Assume that the two groups are geographically separable, with the West having the current-account deficit and the East the current-account surplus. To make the analysis simple, let us also assume, to begin with, that the system as a whole is stationary, with the stock of assets constant, net saving zero, and no capital accumulation. This assumption will be dropped at the end of section B.

A. THE IDEAL SITUATION

In a stationary state, Westerners will gradually draw down their assets to finance their deficits; Easterners will accumulate out of their surpluses. It is also likely that both groups should keep their holdings of money virtually unchanged and wish primarily to draw down or add to their holdings of other financial assets, considering that desired money holdings depend more on flows of income and spending than on the stock of asset holdings, and that they have not changed much. What this will do to the economies of East and West depends on how acceptable to Easterners are the assets Westerners must sell. The ideal situation would be one where the assets Easterners want to buy were exactly the same as those Westerners want to sell. Asset prices would then remain unchanged, the two economies would be unaffected; and the net balance of total payments (other than money) between East and West would be in equilibrium, with equality between autonomous payments and autonomous receipts; because the net current-account disequilibrium in each part of the country would be exactly matched by an offsetting net balance between autonomous payments and receipts on the asset account.

Moreover, this situation would be self correcting also in the long-run, because as Westerners drew down their assets and Easterners built up theirs, each would be impelled to bring its current expenditures more into line with current receipts. Householders accumulating assets would be encouraged thereby to spend more or earn less, those drawing down assets would be forced to cut spending or try to raise their earnings; similarly, firms losing assets would be under pressure either to cut costs through increased efficiency or to raise receipts by making a greater sales effort, improving their product, or developing and marketing new products.

Such adjustments have repercussions on others and so generate multiplier effects on income. When one person eliminates his excess expenditure by reducing his spending, he also reduces some other people's incomes, inducing them to lower also their spending and so reduce still other people's incomes in turn. But these effects will be offset, at least partly, by the actions of those who eliminate their excess expenditures by raising their receipts and so generate repercussions in the opposite direction. Firms, for example, that eliminate their deficits by increasing sales often generate an upward cumulative effect capable of offsetting and nullifying the downward multiplier effect of other firms' and people's cuts in spending.[1] Long-run

[1]This will happen if they increase their sales by increasing their customers' propensity to spend, or, at the least, their propensity to spend on Western products. See section B of chapter 9 below for a more detailed discussion of this case and of the entire argument that an excess of expenditures may be eliminated without a general, multiplier-induced fall in incomes.

equilibrium therefore, with equality between autonomous payments and autonomous receipts separately on both the current and the asset account, may come about without a cumulative multiplier process and with a minimum change in incomes and expenditures beyond that directly created by those eliminating a disequilibrium between their receipts and payments.

The situation just described was one of balance-of-payments disequilibrium ideally resolved in both the short and the long run solely through the changed behavior of people and firms attending to their individual financial situations under pressures no greater than what changes in the physical quantities of their asset holdings put on them, with virtually no price and only small income changes and with no need for the authorities to intervene. This ideal adjustment process, which involves no problems and creates no payments difficulties, will be our standard of perfection in what follows. We shall be concerned with two questions: the conditions of attaining this ideal, and the consequences of not attaining it.

A necessary condition of realizing this ideal situation would be the perfect integration between East and West of the markets for all assets liable to be bought and sold in the two areas in response to imbalances between payments and receipts. Since we do not know which these assets are, it is easier to deal with the sufficient condition that the markets for *all* assets be perfectly integrated. The perfect integration of asset markets means, in this context, that the assets must be transferable and the portfolio preferences of individual asset holders regionally unbiased. In other words, neither Easterners nor Westerners must have a preference for assets of their own area on grounds of local patriotism, convenience, or their greater familiarity with and better judgment of the local scene.

Let it be said right away that this is as unattainable an ideal and as purely theoretical a construction as perfect competition. In none but the smallest communities have all asset markets ever been completely integrated; but even partial fulfilment of these conditions can go a long way toward solving balance-of-payments problems. This will be illustrated in section C by a discussion of regional payments adjustment within the United States. At first, however, we must try to analyze what happens when the condition of the perfect integration of all asset markets is not fulfilled.

B. THE GENERAL CASE

When the West is in current-account deficit and the East in surplus, transferable assets (e.g., stocks and bonds, and Government bonds and bills) sold in the West will be bought up in the East, with no need nor even much likelihood of changes in their prices. Western orders to sell will be counterbalanced by Eastern orders to buy; and the Eastward movement of these securities will easily pay for a part of the Westward excess flow on current account.

At the same time, however, Westerners will also try to sell, and Easterners to buy, assets that cannot or cannot easily move from West to East at their pre-existing prices. The prices of these *will* be affected, falling in the West and rising in the East. Similarly, bank balances will be drawn down in the West and built up in the East, causing Western banks to lose reserves and Eastern banks to gain them. When they try to restore their reserve ratios and adjust their holdings of non-liquid assets, the banks will find themselves in the same position as their customers: able to buy and sell transferable assets without affecting their prices but not able to do this with others. Indeed, the unresponsiveness of an asset's price to selling in one and buying in another region is the best index of the degree to which its market is integrated. The unresponsiveness of asset prices as a whole to asset transfers and attempted asset transfers of this sort indicates the extent of integration of asset markets in general.

The prices of the non-transferable assets change in both Western and Eastern markets, because at ruling prices there are sellers only in the West and buyers only in the East. Their prices therefore must fall in the West and rise in the East, until Western asset holders are induced to concentrate their sales, and Eastern asset holders their purchases, on *transferable* assets alone. In other words, when not all the assets are transferable that Westerners in deficit want to sell and Easterners in surplus want to buy, then relative asset prices change until *all* the assets released in the West and absorbed in the East are rendered transferable and their transfer is capable to offset fully the current-account imbalance between East and West. This is accomplished mainly by the change in the price of non-transferable assets rendering inopportune their sale in the West and their purchase in the East, and to a lesser extent also by the fall in price of the West's non-transferable assets rendering some of them transferable—that is, attractive enough for Easterners to acquire.

The release, transfer, and absorption, of enough transferable assets to offset fully the current-account imbalance will be accomplished with the less change in the prices of non-transferable assets, the smaller the proportion of these in the total stock of assets and the greater the elasticity of substitution between them and transferable assets. This also implies that the prices of non-transferable assets must continue to fall in the West and to rise in the East as the Westward excess flow of products persists, because the offsetting Eastward flow of transferable assets makes their proportion diminish in Western and rise in Eastern portfolios. This means that to assure the continuation of a given Eastward flow of transferable assets requires further and further changes in the prices of the other assets.

While these changes in asset prices are an accompaniment and condition of the short-run balancing of the current-account imbalance by the offsetting flow of transferable assets, they also have a great impact on long-run adjustment. In the ideal situation, only the depletion of Western and expansion of Eastern portfolios would put pressure on asset holders to bring their current payments into harmony with their receipts and so stop further changes in their asset holdings; here, that pressure is reinforced by strong additional pressures on them resulting from changes in the market value of the non-transferable part of their portfolios—capital losses in the West and capital gains in the East. Such additional pressure is needed, of course, because the smaller the transferable part of asset holdings, the sooner must long-run equilibrium be restored and short-run offsetting of excess product flows by equilibrating asset flows be brought to an end.

A further and even more important consequence of the changes in asset prices is their impact on the general level of incomes, employment and commodity prices. The fall in the prices of local assets in the West will depress incomes, because it is equivalent to a rise in interest rates and a stiffening of the terms of credit, which will discourage investment, restrict housing construction and consumer buying on credit, and so lower general economic activity, employment and to a limited extent perhaps also commodity prices. In the East, the opposite pressures are exerted by the rise in the prices of local assets, often with a greater impact on commodity prices in view of their greater upward flexibility.

The role of these changes in restoring current-account equilibrium is obvious. The fall of incomes in the West will reduce the Westward flow of goods and services by an amount equal to this fall times the West's marginal propensity to import; the rise of incomes in the East will exert a corresponding stimulus on the Eastward flow of products; and to the extent that commodity prices, too, have changed, they will further inhibit the Westward and encourage the Eastward flow of products.

We have, then, three forces tending to restore equilibrium on the current account of the balance of payments. Changes in the physical quantity of (transferable) assets in people's and firms' portfolios, changes in the market value of (non-transferable) assets, and changes in the level of income and employment. The first and second exert their influence on individual behavior through the pressure of changing wealth, the third through the pressure of changing incomes, employment and commodity prices—a crucial distinction, since changes in income and employment have important social and human implications that changes in wealth largely lack. The first equilibrating force alone would be present in the ideal situation, with all assets transferable; only when some assets are not transferable do the second and third emerge, and their relative importance increases with the proportion of such assets in the total stock of all assets.

This is the reason why the ideal situation would be ideal. It is true that long-run adjustment must be made even in the ideal situation, and that this probably involves some income changes even then; but these would be milder and more gradual under the impact of changing assets positions alone; and besides, the cumulative deflationary process in the West is likely to be less or even altogether absent in that case.[2]

Our distinguishing between the three forces of long-run adjustment should also serve as a reminder as to what exactly long-run equilibrium means in the present context. It was defined solely in relation to the balance of payments as a situation of rest that can persist indefinitely, in so far that—with equilibrium on the current account—it involves a drawing down or accumulation neither of official reserves

[2]Cf. pp. 88–89 above and also section B of chapter 9 below.

nor of privately held assets. From the domestic point of view, however, of the areas in question, this need not necessarily be a satisfactory state of affairs, since it may involve (and hinge on!) underemployment in one of the areas. The possibility of conflict between payments (or external) equilibrium on the one hand and domestic equilibrium on the other will be dealt with in chapter 12, in our discussion of problems of policy. Here, where our concern is with automatic payments adjustment, we only note that once long-run equilibrium is established, the equilibrating forces are spent—with perhaps one exception. When to restore payments equilibrium between two areas requires underemployment and depression in one and inflationary pressures in the other, and labor is free to migrate between them, the movement of labor might help to restore domestic equilibrium in both areas.[3]

So far we were concerned with the stationary state; but it is easy to extend the argument to the progressive economy. Progress in an economy may be thought of as a chronic payments imbalance between the business and the household sector. Capital accumulation in the business sector means an excess of payments over receipts, the sector's import surplus financed by the issue of new assets, which the household sector buys out of its export surplus; that is, out of its saving or its excess of income over expenditures. The continued accumulation of the household sector's savings leads to a secular increase in its expenditures on imports from the business sector, which responds by paying more incomes to the household sector and, if all goes well, by continuing to invest and issue the new assets that the household sector (in view of its rising incomes) will wish to accumulate.

For our purposes, however, we must sector the economy by geographical regions, not by function. East and West are in current-account equilibrium when the deficit of each region's business sector is exactly offset by the surplus of its household sector. If something

[3]It might also help to restore payments equilibrium, since emigration lowers and immigration raises an area's propensity to import. On the other hand, the money and other accumulated savings migrating workers take with them pull the balance of payments in the opposite direction, and so does the influence of labor migration on wages, cost and price levels. It is not likely therefore that the migration of labor should be an important equilibrating force as far as the balance of payments is concerned.

H

disturbs this equilibrium between the two regions, problems arise and equilibrating forces emerge that are identical with those just discussed. An import surplus in the West will be offset by an Eastward flow of assets from the West, promoted to the extent necessary by a fall in the West and rise in the East of the market values of local assets.

In this case, however, the fall in Western asset prices and their depressing effect on investment, consumer spending, and levels of income and employment will not be so strong, because the accumulation of capital creates new assets; among them transferable assets, which can offset their Eastward drain and replenish diminishing portfolios. Nevertheless, a long-run tendency toward current-account equilibrium is likely to be present even in this case. For the Eastward flow of transferable assets will still affect both asset-to-income ratios and the ratio of transferable to local assets in people's portfolios; and if people care about these ratios, their market behavior will show it and push toward long-run equilibrium.

This conclusion parallels the one we reached for the stationary state; but it may hold only if East and West are very similar in terms of household behavior, production conditions, and other economic characteristics. For the history of international economic relations hardly seems to bear out the conclusion that there is a long-run tendency toward current-account equilibrium between different economies. Many a country has been a net exporter or importer of capital for decades, without any apparent tendency toward the elimination of its capital exports or imports. While very little is known about the adjustment mechanism that makes this possible or brings it about, the problem will at least be discussed at a later stage.[4]

C. INTERREGIONAL PAYMENTS ADJUSTMENT IN THE UNITED STATES

It would be refreshing at this stage to shift from theory to practice and see how the automatic payments mechanism really works in an area where it is allowed to operate: between the different regions of the same country. Unfortunately for the professional economist, inter-

[4]Cf. section B of chapter 10 below.

regional payments-adjustment functions so smoothly and perfectly most of the time that the need has not yet arisen to collect statistics and other empirical information on the subject. The following analysis therefore must also be largely speculative.

In small or highly centralized countries, the proportion of transferable assets in the total is presumably very high and interregional payments adjustment probably approaches our ideal case quite closely. But even in a country as large and decentralized as the United States, the mechanism seems remarkably smooth and painless.[5]

It has been estimated that of the total stock of all financial assets in the United States, about one third has a nationwide market.[6] This one third was worth, in 1958 (the latest year for which asset estimates are available), around $700 billion, or almost twice the annual national income; and it comprizes, among other assets, central-bank money (cash and Federal Funds), all Federal securities other than special issues, most State, local and corporate bonds, and about two-thirds of all corporate stock. Experience suggests that this volume of nationally marketable and transferable assets is enough to handle interregional payments and resolve interregional payments imbalance in the United States almost as perfectly as the ideal system would.

With transferable assets a third of the total stock of the country's financial assets, it is not surprising that very small changes in the prices of only locally marketable assets should be enough to bring about the release, transfer, and absorption of sufficient transferable assets to offset all imbalances between regions on the current account.

To begin with, quite apart from and before any changes in asset prices, not many only locally marketable assets are of the kind people and firms would first think of selling or buying in response to an imbalance between their receipts and expenditures. Excluded from the outset are most real assets, perhaps also most very illiquid assets; and there is bound to be a correlation between liquidity and nationwide marketability. In short, considerations of convenience already bias asset sales and purchases in favor of those nationally marketable.

[5]This, however, has not always been so. Even as late as the great depression of the 1930's, there were regional outbreaks of bank failures of epidemic proportions; and bank failures, when primarily due to illiquidity, are the original and classic form of balance-of-payments difficulties.

[6]By Prof. R. W. Goldsmith in private correspondence with the author.

Furthermore, nationally marketable assets and assets marketable only locally exist side-by-side in virtually every category of assets, from bonds to bills and from equities to mortgages; and this makes for a high elasticity and great ease of substitution between nationally and locally marketable assets. Small changes in the latter's prices therefore can cause great shifts in preferences. Lastly, most of the commercial banks' portfolio of securities is nationally marketable, which means that interregional shifts in customers' deposits can be effected with a minimum of dislocation and pressure on the banks to contract or expand their credit. In other words, when it comes to making payments in other regions of the country, most of the banks' investments in securities are, in effect, part of their reserves.[7]

Here then is a large part of the explanation of why balance-of-payments equilibrium is so easily and automatically maintained between different regions of the United States. Any imbalance between one region's exports and imports is automatically balanced by an offsetting imbalance between that region's inflow and outflow of assets. The reason why autonomous capital flows providentially offset the current-account imbalance is that the latter reflects an equal imbalance between the total receipts and payments of individual persons and firms, who must readjust their asset holdings accordingly and who, partly for convenience, partly prompted by minor changes in relative asset prices, sell and buy primarily those assets that can move between regions. These equilibrating autonomous asset flows explain balance-of-payments equilibrium between the regions of a country in the short run—and the short run in this context can last for years.

But long-run adjustment, too, seems smooth and painless, to judge by appearances. One reason, presumably, is a relatively light reliance on changes in income and heavy reliance on changes in wealth as influences on individual spending behavior, owing to the not-too-high proportion of non-transferable assets in the total. Another, no less important reason must be the fact that payments adjustment *via* changes in income levels is easier and less painful in interregional

[7]Bankers always regard their portfolio of securities as their second line of defense. But these can be liquidated without a capital loss only in connection with interregional transfers, because then, and only then, is the market pressure of bankers trying to sell such securities offset by the market pressure of the other region's bankers trying to buy them.

than in international relations; because to achieve a given improvement in the payments balance requires a lesser change in incomes. It is true that, with the generally greater volume of interregional trade, the needed payments adjustments are also greater; but this is more than offset by the greater ease of interregional payments adjustment.

To illustrate, assume that while a country's imports from abroad are 5 per cent of her total income, the imports of her Western region from the country's other regions are 50 per cent of its (the Western region's) total income, and that their marginal propensities to import are also .05 and .5 respectively. Assume further that the typical payments deficit of each is 1/10 of imports. In other words, the country's typical payments deficit with the outside world is ½ of 1 per cent of the national income, that of the West with the rest of the country is 5 per cent of its total income. To remove a typical payments deficit therefore, the country's income would have to be reduced by 10 per cent, $\frac{1}{.05}$ times the desired ½ of 1 per cent reduction in imports; and the West's income would also have to be reduced by 10 per cent, $\frac{1}{.5}$ times the desired 5 per cent reduction in its imports. The greater size of a region's typical payments imbalance exactly offsets the greater response of its imports to changes in income.

This, however, is not the end of the story. A reduction in a region's income improves its balance of payments not only because it lowers its imports but also because it lowers its tax and social insurance payments to central Government which from its point of view are external payments, just as imports are.[8] The full response therefore of a region's external payments to a change in its income will be this change times the sum of its marginal propensity to import *and* its marginal propensity to pay taxes and tax-like contributions to central Government.

The last factor may well enhance this response by one-third, and so reduce by one-quarter the change in regional incomes necessary to bring about a given change in interregional payments—considering that the marginal propensity to pay taxes to central Government is

[8]This is so, because the volume and regional distribution of a central Government's expenditures are determined independently of its receipts from a particular region.

around twenty to twenty-five per cent in most developed countries, while the marginal propensity to import from other regions is at most three times as great.

An additional and similar factor is the tendency of central Government and Government agencies to increase their payments in, and so add to the external receipts of, regions whose income is falling. Unemployment compensation is one example, the policy to concentrate public investment and defense contracts in regions most in need of additional employment is another, farm price supports is a third. This factor, together with the previous one, explains the greater efficacy and ease of payments adjustment *via* income changes in interregional relations; and it is the second part of the explanation of why interregional payments adjustment in the United States is as smooth and painless as it is.[9]

D. PAYMENTS ADJUSTMENT UNDER THE CLASSICAL GOLD STANDARD

The foregoing argument should have made amply clear that the market economy generates adequate equilibrating forces for maintaining payments equilibrium between different geographical areas as long as all its members, including households, firms, financial intermediaries, *and authorities,* maintain their individual payments balances. Balance-of-payments problems and difficulties of adjustment between nations arise because this last condition is not fulfilled: the authorities do not "play the game." For this there can be many reasons; in the following we shall merely try to show the presence and adequacy of one reason: the very much greater and probably intolerable burden that payments adjustment would impose if the equilibrating forces just described were fully relied upon and given free play in the international sphere. To show that this is so, we shall try to see what would happen if the adjustment mechanism just described were to operate also between countries; in other words, if the classical gold standard were to operate today as it operated in its heyday—or rather, as most present-day economists believe it operated in its heyday.

[9]For the third explanation, see section B of chapter 9.

For the classical gold standard was neither more nor less than a complete reliance in the realm of international economic relations on the equilibrating market forces here analyzed. This was accomplished, or perhaps only supposed to be accomplished, by the simple device of requiring the central bank of every country that had one to obey rules that made it behave exactly as commercial banks behave. In other words, each central bank was expected, not to pursue an independent monetary policy, but to maintain in fairly mechanical fashion a prescribed relation, usually a stable ratio, between its reserves and the sum of currency issued and its customers' (the commercial banks') deposits.

We saw in section A of chapter 3 that such behavior by commercial banks creates a credit multiplier and gives the central bank, which controls the volume of commercial-bank reserves, a leverage in influencing the amount of money and credit in the economy. Now, if the central bank also maintained a fixed ratio between its reserves and liabilities, this would create another credit multiplier and give leverage in influencing the volume of *cash* to whoever or whatever determined the volume of central-bank reserves. Moreover, since part of this cash constitutes the commercial banks' reserves, the two credit multipliers would be superimposed and give a correspondingly greater leverage to changes in central-bank reserves in influencing the supply of money and credit in the economy.

The relevance of all this lies, of course, in the fact that the reserves of the central bank are at the same time the external reserves of the country. Under the classical gold standard therefore, with central bank and commercial banks obeying the same rules of banking, changes in the country's external reserves called for proportionate but greater changes in the supply of money, the achievement of which required constant readjustments in the conditions and volume of credit offered by the banking system. Such readjustments were an integral part of the automatic equilibrating mechanism; but they could be painful, not only in forcing drastic changes in the level of employment and activity, but sometimes even to the point of precipitating bankruptcies and so preventing readjustment.

The main determinant of the ease or difficulty, both of such readjustments and of the overall operation of the entire adjustment mechanism, is the proportion of internationally transferable assets held by a country's residents and authorities. The proportion of the central bank's holdings of external reserves determines the leverage of the credit multiplier; other internationally transferable assets and external reserves held elsewhere in the economy reduce the need for central-bank reserves to finance payments deficits and so diminish reliance on the credit multiplier for long-run adjustment.

Among internationally transferable assets one ought to list a country's official and unofficial external reserves,[10] foreign and international assets held by residents (though not the direct investments abroad of domestic corporations, which are not easily transferable and negotiable), and the domestically held domestic securities which have an additional market established abroad. Statistics are available for all countries on the first item, for some on the second, for none on the third. The volume of this last is probably still small today but growing. The market for the shares of the large international corporations is getting as international as their scale of operations, the stock even of some non-international U.S. companies is saleable abroad, and members of the European Economic Community are increasingly trading in each other's securities. All these had to be left out, for lack of data, from the table, which shows, for selected countries, the first two items only.[11] At the same time, however, even this incomplete listing of internationally transferable assets overstates, in a sense, the volume of those available for equilibrating transfers. For in today's uneasy world, fears of devaluation or exchange control are never completely absent in any country with payments difficulties. When such fears become acute, they render privately held foreign assets especially attractive to their holders and the country's domestic assets especially unattractive to foreigners. This means that in case of need, privately held assets cease to be available for equilibrating international transfers in response to price changes. It would not be far off the mark therefore to regard external reserves alone as internationally transferable assets.

In the table, a more optimistic view is taken and the volume of internationally transferable assets is shown for nine countries on a broad definition that includes official and unofficial reserves, foreign

[10]I.e., reserves held by the central bank and those held by others, chiefly commercial banks and other financial intermediaries.

[11]For most countries not shown here, the second item is not available and not significant, reserves forming the bulk of their transferable assets.

assets in private portfolios and private hoards of gold. This total is also shown as the ratio that it bears, in each country, to the estimated volume of the country's nationally transferable assets. This latter has been estimated on the assumption that in all the countries here considered, it bears the same ratio to national income as it did in the United States in 1958, the year for which the estimate quoted on p. 95 is available. This is, of course, very approximate; but it seemed a reasonable assumption to make also for the other countries. It is true that the proportion of nationally marketable assets in the total may be much higher in these countries than in the United States; on the other hand, their gross stock of financial assets is probably a lower multiple of the national income.[12] If the two errors do not cancel each other, the ratios are likely to err on the high side, which (in this context) is the conservative side. The estimates are crude but do indicate orders of magnitude.

The table shows that with the single exception of Switzerland, the volume of internationally transferable financial assets tends to be a small fraction of the volume of interregionally transferable assets, 1/10 and 1/15 are typical orders of magnitude.

A volume of internationally transferable assets that is 1/10 or 1/15 of the volume of interregionally transferable assets does not quite mean 10 or 15 times greater strains and burdens of balance-of-payments adjustment. For the ratio of international trade in the total volume of trade is also smaller than the ratio of interregional trade to total trade, owing to greater distances and trade restrictions, many of the latter imposed in order to ease such strains. The disparity, however, in the volume of transferable assets is many times greater, perhaps four to six times as great as the disparity in the volume of trade —and such 'net disparity' *can* be regarded as a rough measure of the greater burden of international balance-of-payments adjustment.[13]

[12]Because credit is less used and the market for capital less highly developed in most countries than in the United States.

[13]It is difficult to estimate the net disparity, because we have no statistics of the volume of interregional trade. The European Economic Community, when it reaches the ultimate stage of the complete freeing of trade among member countries, will furnish evidence on the disparity in volume between international and interregional trade. At the time of writing (1966), intra-Community trade can be estimated at 70 per cent higher than what it would be had the Community never been established.

THE VOLUME OF TRANSFERABLE ASSETS

(In billions of U.S. dollars)
mid-1966

	Canada	*Belgium*	*France*	*Germany*	*Italy*	*Netherlands*	*Switzerland*	*U.K.*	*U.S.A.*
Official reserves	2.8	2.3	6.9	7.7	4.4	2.3	3.0	3.2	15.2
Unofficial reserves	—	.2	—	1.0	2.5	1.7	—	—	.5
Foreign assets in private portfolios	1.8	?	1.0*	1.3**	?	.5†	9.2	10.1	31.7
Private hoards of gold			4.5††						
All internationally transferable assets	4.6	2.5	12.4	10.0	6.9	4.5	12.2	13.3	47.4
Nationally transferable assets	(69)	(26)	(123)	(150)	(87)	(30)	(20)	(140)	(1100)
Ratio of internationally to nationally transferable assets	1/15	1/10	1/10	1/15	1/13	1/7	3/5	1/11	1/23

* Estimated from dividend income.

** Cumulated sum of net annual acquisitions. Does not include capital gains.

† Holdings of investment trusts only.

†† Estimated in "Pick's World Currency Reports." Holdings in the other countries are generally believed to be very much smaller.

The significance of this net disparity is, first, that if the automatic equilibrating forces were given full sway in international relations, international payments adjustment would have to be four to six times less gradual than interregional payments adjustment, in view of the that many times smaller ratio of assets usable for equilibrating transfers. In other words, the short run, in which asset movements assure payments equilibrium, would have to be abbreviated four- to six-fold and long-run adjustment speeded up accordingly. Moreover, this speeding up of long-run adjustment would be (and could only be) achieved by a corresponding increase in the relative importance of changing asset prices and income levels as equilibrating forces.

It is especially this latter that might render intolerable the strain of payments adjustment, the more so, because the leverage of income changes as an equilibrating force is also significantly smaller in international than in interregional relations. All this might necessitate incessant and violent fluctuations in income, employment and prices, the cost of which, in terms of economic dislocation and human suffering, would probably far outweigh the advantages of international specialization and trade.[14]

David Hume, two-hundred years ago, described essentially the same payments equilibrating mechanism discussed in this chapter but without any mention of burdens and costs of adjustment; believing, perhaps rightly under the conditions of his age, that changes in money income would reflect changes in prices rather than employment and therefore involve a much lesser cost. It is also possible that the difference in volume between regionally and nationally transferable assets was also much smaller in his time, which developed the machinery of international finance far ahead of its national counterpart.

Today, the equilibrating forces discussed in this chapter hardly operate in the realm of international payments, because one member of each economy, its central bank, does not behave as a private bank would and does not maintain a stable ratio between reserves and liabilities; and the central bank is not only an important holder of assets but the main, often the only repository of external reserves.

[14]One must also recall that as soon as the strain of payments adjustment engenders fears of devaluation or exchange control, private holdings of internationally transferable assets become unavailable for equilibrating transfers; and this greatly increases the strain.

Central banks used to be held, as other financial intermediaries still are, to maintaining a stable ratio between their (external) reserves and their liabilities. By not maintaining nor even trying to maintain this ratio, they ease the pressure of equilibrating forces on asset prices and interest rates, and through them on income and price levels, by a factor that is the reciprocal of this ratio. More exactly, if the initial ratio of a central bank's holdings of external reserves to its liabilities (i.e., central-bank money outstanding) would be .25, and if these were the country's only internationally transferable assets, then, if the central bank pursued no active policy to maintain this ratio, its inaction would diminish the pressure of equilibrating forces four-fold.

Moreover, central banks often pursue an active policy in the opposite direction, calculated to *offset* the market's equilibrating forces, with a view to relieving their pressure also on the commercial banking system or on the economy as a whole.

Whenever the central bank's policy weakens or offsets the pressure of equilibrating market forces, balance-of-payments problems and difficulties for the authorities to resolve can arise. It is these that call for deliberate balance-of-payments equilibrating policies.

Bibliography to Chapter 8

The main sources for this chapter were J. C. Ingram, *Regional Payments Mechanisms: The Case of Puerto Rico* (Univ. of North Carolina Press, 1962); Part II of my *Economic Theory and Western European Integration* (Stanford Univ. Press, 1958); and R. J. Hawtrey, *The Art of Central Banking.*

Chapter 9

Sources of imbalance —shifts in demand

The last chapter, besides posing the general problem of the balance of payments, presented the classical theory of the forces of balance-of-payments adjustment, known in a rudimentary form already to David Hume. But the movement of assets, and the changes in wealth and income brought about by the sale and purchase of assets, are not the only forces of payment adjustment. Sometimes the very change in conditions that disrupts an initial balance also generates equilibrating forces, quite separate from and additional to those just discussed. For a complete analysis of the subject, these too must be taken into account. They are known as payments adjustment by income changes; sometimes also called the Keynesian adjustment mechanism.[1] Moreover, since not every disruption of the balance of payments generates these forces, to know when and how they arise is as important as to know the way they operate. In this and the next two chapters therefore we shall deal with the separate problems and resolutions of

[1]The Keynesian theory of payments adjustment is a simple extension of Keynesian multiplier theory to an open economy, whence the name. Keynes himself, however, never stated the "Keynesian" theory of payments adjustment; as a matter of fact, at an early stage he even argued against a forerunner of what we now call his theory.

problems created by each of the three types of balance-of-payments disturbance. The first of these is a shift in demand. This, together with certain capital transfers, is the only payments disturbance directly to generate payments equilibrating forces.

A. KEYNESIAN PAYMENTS ADJUSTMENT BY INCOME CHANGES

Consider that the consuming public shifts its custom from one seller to another by ΔZ. This will lower the flow of the first seller's receipts and raise the second seller's by ΔZ but will change the balance of their receipts and payments by a lesser amount. For both sellers' outlays are likely to be affected by the change in their receipts; and if we designate by e their marginal propensities to spend out of receipts, then the worsening of the first and improvement of the second seller's balance of payments will only be

$$(1 - e)\Delta Z.$$

These changes in their respective balances of payments are the only consequence of the shift in consumers' tastes if both are members of the same economy and located close to each other, because then, the effect of the first seller's diminished expenditure on the rest of the world will be offset by the additional expenditure of the second.

Assume next that the two sellers inhabit different parts of the world, the first the North, the second the South. We will then want to know how the shift in demand affects the balance of payments between North and South. For this purpose, we must separate the marginal propensity to spend into two components: the propensity to spend on domestic and the propensity to spend on foreign goods; and we shall assume that they bear the relation

$$d + f = e < 1.$$

We shall distinguish the propensities of North and South by subscripts and assume that all inhabitants of the same region have the same propensities. It is immaterial for the argument whether the consumers who shift their custom are from the North, the South, or from both, although ΔZ will denote an increase in North's imports in the first case, a reduction in her exports in the second, and a combination of the two in the third.

North's incomes will fall in any case, partly because ΔZ represents a fall of incomes in her export and/or import-competing industries, and partly because the impact of this fall on domestic spending will lower incomes yet further. In symbols:

$$\Delta Y_n = -\Delta Z + d_n \Delta Y_n.$$

Collecting and rearranging terms, the total fall in North's income appears as

$$\Delta Y_n = -\frac{1}{1-d_n}\Delta Z;$$

and the induced fall in its imports as

$$\Delta F_n = -\frac{f_n}{1-d_n}\Delta Z.$$

Let us denote the response of a group's imports to an autonomous change in the outside world's effective demand for its output by the symbol g, so that

$$g_n = \frac{f_n}{1-d_n}.$$

It is worth noting that g has the same meaning for a group that e, the marginal propensity to spend, has for an individual; and that

$$g = e \qquad \text{when} \qquad e = 1 \qquad \text{and}$$

$$g < e \qquad \text{whenever} \qquad e < 1.$$[2]

The shift in tastes, which would worsen North's balance of payments by ΔZ if incomes remained unchanged, will worsen it only by

(1) $(1 - g_n)\,\Delta Z$

if incomes in the North are affected by the change in demand and allowed to respond.

The way in which incomes in the two areas are affected is shown by the two simultaneous equations:

$$(1-d_n)\Delta Y_n - f_s \Delta Y_s = -\Delta Z$$

$$-f_n \Delta Y_n + (1-d_s)\Delta Y_s = \Delta Z.$$

[2]Note that

$$e - g = \frac{d}{1-d}(1-d-f) = \frac{d}{1-d}(1-e).$$

Their solution shows the change in each area's incomes:

$$\Delta Y_n = -\frac{1 - d_s - f_s}{D} \Delta Z, \qquad \Delta Y_s = \frac{1 - d_n - f_n}{D} \Delta Z,$$

where $$D = (1 - d_n)(1 - d_s) - f_n f_s.$$

From this one easily obtains the change in each area's induced imports, shown by the expressions:

$$\Delta F_n = -\frac{(1 - d_s - f_s)f_n}{D} \Delta Z, \qquad \Delta F_s = \frac{(1 - d_n - f_n)f_s}{D} \Delta Z.$$

Adding these to the initial shift in demand yields the total change in the balance of payments between the two areas:

$$\Delta B = \Delta Z - \Delta F_n + \Delta F_s.$$

After some rearrangement, this can also be written as:

(1) $$\Delta B = \frac{(1 - g_n)(1 - g_s)}{1 - g_n g_s} \Delta Z.$$

It is apparent that

$$\frac{(1 - g_n)(1 - g_s)}{1 - g_n g_s} \Delta Z < (1 - g) \Delta Z < \Delta Z,$$

which shows that the response of incomes and imports to the shift in demand is an equilibrating force. The balance of payments will be changed, or thrown out of balance, by less if either area's income responds, and by even less if both areas' income levels are affected. The equilibrating force is the more powerful, the higher the values of g; it would completely offset the effect of the shift in demand on the balance of payments if either g_n or g_s were unity.

The value of g may approach unity when the shift in demand affects prices and nominal, rather than real, income. The argument so far was based on the tacit assumption of real incomes' changing and price levels' remaining unaffected. Let us now reverse this assumption at least for the South, assuming full employment in the South, so that the shift in demand in favor of her export or import-competing industries raises money incomes and prices but leaves real incomes unchanged. In this case, f_s and d_s cease to be real propensities and show instead the public's responses to changes in nominal income. As a result, f_s is bound to be higher, since now, besides the rise in money income, the rise in domestic prices relatively to foreign prices provides an additional inducement to import. Similarly, d_s will also be higher, with the sum of f_s and d_s approaching unity, because, when prices rise in proportion with incomes, the rational thing to do is to keep one's real spending unchanged by raising one's nominal spending in proportion with the rise in prices. And, with $(f + d)$ approaching unity, g too approaches unity.[3]

Apart from the special case, however, when the change in incomes is purely nominal, the value of g is likely to be less than one, though it is the higher, the more dependent economically is the area on the outside world. For a country as dependent on foreign trade as the Netherlands, it may reach .5; for a country like the United States, its value is probably around .1. Too much reliance must not be placed therefore on the automatic offsetting of a payments disturbance by the changes in income directly generated by the cause of this disturbance.

B. PAYMENTS ADJUSTMENT WITHOUT INCOME CHANGES

The foregoing argument has shown that a payments disturbance caused by a shift in demand requires a lesser equilibrating movement of assets than might be expected, because the income changes generated by the shift in demand in the regions or countries affected will already influence their imports in an equilibrating direction though not generally to a fully equilibrating extent. These changes in incomes may, of course, be unwelcome in either or both areas affected and call forth domestic stabilizing policies which, if effective, may prevent the income changes and with them also their equilibrating effect on the balance of payments.

This raises an important question, which merits further investigation. We assumed that an initial fall in the effective demand for

[3]The argument of this paragraph is somewhat impressionistic and unrigorous. This analytical approach should not really be used when dealing with a change in nominal incomes, because the arguments that real incomes remain unchanged and that import prices rise less than domestic prices are inconsistent.

North's and rise in that for South's output will have a downward multiplier effect in the North and an upward one in the South, through the well-known Keynesian mechanism that a change in effective demand means an equivalent change in income, which prompts a further though smaller change in effective demand, again implying an equivalent change in income, prompting a yet further change in effective demand, and so *ad infinitum*. This argument tacitly assumes that consumers and producers alike accept passively, and regard as unalterable, changes in their *receipts* and respond to them by appropriately adjusting their *expenditures*. Such an assumption is quite valid and legitimate in the context of Keynesian employment theory; it is neither self evident nor always true in interregional and international trade, as we hope to show below.

In general, one can respond to a fall in one's receipts by reducing one's expenditures; but one can also respond by trying to raise or prevent the fall in one's receipts. American households, for example, are known often to respond to an excess of family expenditures by the wife's taking a job or the husband's moonlighting, rather than by a tightening of the family's belt. Why then do economists always make the opposite assumption in aggregate analysis? The answer, in this example, is that while an individual family may be free to choose between cutting expenditures and supplementing the family's income, households as a group have no such choice, because their total income is limited by employers' effective demand for their services, which, it is reasonable to assume, they cannot influence. As a group therefore they can respond to a fall in their incomes only by cutting their expenditures.

This conclusion, however, hinges on the passive and dependent role members of households play in the labor market, which is very different from the position of producers in product markets. In reacting to a fall in their sales receipts, producers can either accept this as inevitable and reduce output and business outlays correspondingly, or they can respond aggressively by improving their products, developing and marketing new products, lowering price, or stepping up their sales effort in any other way. Unlike householders, producers have this choice not only individually but very often also as a group. While the total sales receipts of all producers is limited by their customers' and potential customers' effective demand, producers can do much to raise their customers' effective demand; and besides, this is not a limiting factor when the question at issue, as here, is the diversion or rediversion of demand from the producers of one geographic area to those of another.[4] It depends entirely on circumstances therefore how producers will react to a fall in their receipts.

Faced with a general downward trend in output and incomes, producers might well be expected to be prudent and choose the passive response of reducing output and business outlays. This is the case assumed and discussed by Keynes when, in the *General Theory,* he deals with the problems of a closed economy. But is this the right assumption to make about producers' response to a fall in sales in our case, where there is no all-pervading gloom in the business outlook and all that has happened is a shift in demand for *some* products in a *part* of the market? In such a case, some, perhaps most producers may be expected to respond aggressively to the decline in their sales; and to the extent that this happens, the tidy conclusions of the previous section need to be modified.

To begin with, the payments adjustment mechanism in the North operates through a fall in incomes; but the higher the proportion of producers who respond aggressively to the fall in their sales, the less will Northern incomes fall; in the limiting case, incomes would not fall at all. A lesser fall in North's incomes will lead to a correspondingly lesser fall in North's imports, and a lesser readjustment of the balance of payments, *given the marginal propensities to import.* On the other hand, the Northern producers' aggressive responses might well change both North's and South's marginal propensities to import, lowering the former, raising the latter, and improving North's balance of payments either way. This means that producers' aggressive reactions to a fall in their sales can accomplish payments adjustment in response to the initial worsening in North's balance of payments *without the painful expedient of lowered incomes and employment.* Whether they will actually do this depends clearly on whether the aggressive Northern producers' sales efforts succeed in diverting their Southern and/or Northern customers' expenditures from Southern products.

There are two cases in which this is likely to happen and this desirable type of payments adjustment is likely to prevail. First, when

[4]What matters is that the Northern producers' aggressive response should raise effective demand *for Northern products.*

the diversion of demand from North's to South's products causes Northern producers to make a deliberate (and successful!) effort to regain the very markets slipping from their grip: a good example is the development of compact cars by the U.S. automobile industry at the end of the 1950's in direct response to the competition of small European cars; but it is hard to specify the general conditions that favor such a response.

The other case is where the export market is a sufficiently important part of the producer's total market for any and every sales effort automatically to be extended to it; and where, at the same time, imports are a sufficiently important part of every buyer's total purchases for most changes in his buying habits or sources of supply automatically to affect imports as well. These conditions are the most likely to obtain, and for obvious reasons, in a region or economy well integrated with other regions or economies. As a matter of fact, an economy's integration with other economies may well favor the first case too. Most businessmen aspire to know, judge, and manipulate the national market they face, and even to anticipate its changing temper; but few will venture aggressive and risky policies beyond its confines. They are more likely therefore to respond aggressively to a loss of markets inside than outside national frontiers, and more likely to direct aggressive sales policies at domestic than at foreign markets.[5] This would imply a greater likelihood both of aggressive producers' responses and of their tendency to improve the payments balance in the case of a region in relation to other regions of the same country than in that of a country in relation to other countries.

To sum up the argument of this and the previous section, we saw that a shift in demand changes the balance of payments between the regions or countries concerned; but the response of consumers and producers to the change in effective demand is able and likely, at least partly, to counterbalance the shift in the payments balance. When this is the passive response familiar from Keynesian multiplier analysis, one can analyze in a rough way the extent to which the fall in incomes in the one and the rise in incomes in the other country or region will lessen the shift in the balance of payments brought about by the initial shift in demand. (This result depends, of course, on incomes being allowed to respond and not being kept from changing

[5]One can respond to a loss of foreign markets by expanding one's domestic market.

by domestic stabilization policies.) On the other hand, when the producers losing demand respond actively, and try to regain their markets or capture others, they will slow or arrest the fall in incomes but without necessarily slowing or arresting the equilibrating adjustment in the balance of payments.

One can now extend this argument. So far we were concerned with the cumulative change in incomes and consequent change in imports occasioned by a shift in demand; but very similar is the fall in incomes and imports that results when a reduced volume or value of asset portfolios discourages householders' spending on consumption and businessmen's on investment. In other words, a deficit country's or region's long-run payments adjustment, brought about by asset movements as described in chapter 8, is very similar to the cumulative process discussed in section A of this chapter. This raises the question: when does the active response of entrepreneurs enable a deficit area to make a long-run payments adjustment without the necessity of a reduction in incomes?

The argument is the same as the one just presented. As long as the restrictive and deflationary pressures are not too great and all-pervasive, there is scope and hope for producers to respond aggressively to the fall in their sales; and when it is a matter of interregional rather than international adjustment, such aggressive response will prevent only the fall in incomes without preventing payments adjustment.

Let us now recall, in the light of this, the argument of chapter 8 concerning long-run adjustment (p. 92). We argued there, that the higher the proportion of transferable assets, the smoother and less painful will be long-run adjustment; because, being less dependent on the restrictive pressure of falling asset prices and rising interest rates, it will be slower and spread out over a longer period. One's instinctive reaction to this argument might well be that it is wrong. If imports and incomes must be reduced by given amounts to restore payments equilibrium, surely it makes little difference, one might argue, whether the same reduction in incomes comes about slowly or fast. But the point is that when incomes are restricted slowly, they need not be restricted by as much. For gentler and slower restrictive pressures, being less pervasive, allow more scope for producers to respond actively to the fall in effective demand they face and so to bring about the same payments adjustment with less change in income.

C. THE TRANSFER PROBLEM

The Keynesian theory of payments adjustment *via* income changes was presented as an account of what happens when people shift their demand, because shifts in demand are an important and frequent cause of payments disturbance. A transfer of capital, however, is somewhat similar in its effects, since it, too, tends directly to create effective demand in the receiving and lower effective demand in the paying country. Indeed, the argument of section A had its origin, in the 1920's and 30's, in the many theoretical discussions of the transfer problem as it was then formulated: could Germany pay the reparations demanded of her after the First World War in the currencies of the victor countries to which they were payable? This required an excess flow of German exports with which to earn the required currencies: what was the machinery to create and maintain this excess flow of products? If the German Government obtained the funds payable by imposing additional taxes on the German public, this would restrict spending in Germany; if the Allied Governments spent the proceeds or used them to remit taxes, spending in their countries would increase; and from here on, further repercussions on incomes in the countries affected would be as analyzed in the case of a shift in demand.

The cumulative fall in incomes and spending in Germany, and their cumulative rise in the Allied countries would, through their respective impacts on German and Allied imports, create an excess flow of products capable of transferring part of the reparation payments, leaving the classical adjustment mechanism of chapter 8 to deal only with the remainder. And if the Germans resented their high taxes or the Allies the expansionary pressures on their economies, they could slow or arrest the changes in incomes and spending, and so hamstring this part of the transfer mechanism.

This argument again suffers from the same shortcomings as the argument of section A. If incomes and spending fall in the paying country (Germany), not only will its imports fall, but domestic producers faced with a shrinking domestic market are quite likely to respond by pushing exports and trying to regain abroad the sales and profits lost at home. If they succeed, they help to create the export surplus needed to accomplish the transfer; but they will also slow the fall in incomes, and with it the fall in imports. In other words, here again the aggressive response of exporters provides a payments adjustment less painful than the Keynesian adjustment *via* income changes and tends to replace rather than to reinforce it.

The only difference between this case and a shift in demand is that the latter changes the current account of the balance of payments, and its income and related effects tend partially to restore the pre-existing balance on the same account; whereas a capital transfer changes the asset account of the balance of payments, and its income and related effects change the current account in a way partially to restore the pre-existing overall balance.

It used to be believed that foreign lending, the other common cause of the international transfer of capital, had similar income effects; but this is only half true. The spending of a foreign loan's proceeds by its recipient does have a stimulating multiplier effect on incomes likely also to raise the receiving country's imports—the more so, because foreign loans are usually obtained for financing investment projects especially dependent on imported equipment, and part of the proceeds tend directly (and are often required) to be spent in the lending country. However, the granting of the loan, i.e., the floating or sale of foreign securities in the lending country, does not have the symmetrical effect of destroying (or diverting) that much effective demand. It may have a damping effect on the lenders' economy, because the offer of additional securities for sale puts a downward pressure on asset prices likely to restrain capital formation and consumer spending; but the magnitude of this or its effects on incomes bears no simple and predictable relation to the value of the loan raised. In short, while the proceeds of the loan are almost certain to be spent, and so to generate and stimulate the further generation of incomes wherever the recipient chooses to spend them; the raising of the loan has only indirect, uncertain and unpredictable, though probably lesser, restraining effects on the lenders' economy. There is no more symmetry in the magnitude of these contrary effects than in their mode of operation.

Bibliography to Chapter 9

The Keynesian or income theory of payments adjustment was probably first stated in F. W. Paish, "Banking Policy and the Balance of International Payments," *Economica,* Vol. 39 (1929) pp. 404–23, and W. A. Salant, "Foreign Trade Policy in the Business Cycle," in *Readings in the Theory of International Trade* (Irwin, 1949). For a modern statement, see H. G. Johnson, *International Trade and Economic Growth* (Allen & Unwin, London, 1958), chapters VI and VII.

For the discussion of payments adjustment through active entrepreneurial responses, see B. J. Cohen, "Adjustment Costs and the Distribution of New Reserves," International Finance Section, Dept. of Economics, Princeton University, and Staffan B. Linder, *An Essay on Trade and Transformation* (Wiley, 1961).

For the transfer problem, see L. A. Metzler, "The Transfer Problem Reconsidered," *Journal of Political Economy,* Vol. 50 (1942) pp. 397–414, and the references there cited.

Chapter 10

Sources of imbalance —cost disparities

In the last chapter we considered those sources of payments disequilibrium whose impact effect on external payments tends to be offset by their income effects so that, on balance, they leave only a residual and lesser disturbance to be resolved by the movement of assets as described in chapter 8. Very different and more severe in their effects on the balance of payments are geographic differences in cost and price levels. High costs and prices relative to costs and prices elsewhere are the most intractable cause of payments difficulties for two reasons. First of all, the income effects of cost divergences not only do not mitigate but reinforce their impact effect on the balance of payments. The impact effect of cost and price levels higher than elsewhere is a price effect, which renders exports dear and imports cheap, and so inhibits the former and encourages the latter. The income effect further encourages imports, since the higher money income created by higher cost levels represents, in relation to imports, a higher real income.

The second and very different kind of reason why disparities in cost levels create intractable payments difficulties is that they can render unsatisfactory and untenable the long-run payments equilibrium discussed in chapter 8. We showed there how equilibrating asset flows, through their influence on wealth and income levels, tend to restore current-account equilibrium between foreign receipts and foreign payments. This, however, is long-run equilibrium only as far as the balance of payments is concerned. It is an unsatisfactory state of affairs from the domestic point of view if to achieve and maintain it requires unemployment—or more unemployment than society is willing to live with. And the likelihood of that is especially great when high price and cost levels create the initial payments disequilibrium, since their all-pervading payments-worsening influence may well need to be balanced by the equally all-pervading payments-improving influence of depression and unemployment.

When wages are rigid downwards, a high-cost area may have no escape from the dilemma of choosing between a payments deficit on the one hand and a payments equilibrium assured by the mutually balancing influences of unemployment and high costs on the other hand. Many a high-cost country has experienced the painful nature of this dilemma, from which the only escape, exchange-rate depreciation, is also beset with obstacles. These will be discussed in section B of chapter 13 below. The question remains, however, why divergences between cost levels and the resulting difficulties are so rare among regions of the same country, which do not have the escape of exchange-rate depreciation. The answer is that there, many factors are at work to keep cost divergences from arising. It will be useful to discuss these in the following.

A. LIMITS TO COST DIVERGENCES BETWEEN REGIONS

The economic integration of geographic areas has three aspects: the free movement of goods, the free movement of labor, and the free movement of assets. All three contribute to limiting divergences in costs. Goods, in a competitive world, move in response to regional differences in their prices; and their movement keeps these differences between the limits set by the cost of transporting them. Indirectly, this also sets limits to divergences of costs between regions. Management in a given region will not concede and labor will not press too hard for wages that would push costs beyond these limits, the former for fear of diminishing profits, the latter for fear of diminishing employment. The pressure of such competition is the greater the more the area depends on and competes with the outside world, which is one reason why such competition is so much more effective within an integrated economy than between different economies. The other and no less important reason is the absence, within an integrated economy, of independent regional employment policies, which could mitigate or obviate the effects of a wage increase on profits and employment. This will be discussed further when we deal with the mobility of assets, the main factor that rules out regional employment policies.

The mobility of labor is never so great, and its market never so perfect as that of goods; on the other hand, regional wage differentials are a direct inducement for labor to move, and the movement of labor sets a direct limit to wage differentials. Also, while goods have to keep moving in a continuous flow to keep price divergences within limits, labor has to move only once to bring about a permanent reduction in wage differences. All this renders interregional labor mobility an important force to keep regional wage differentials within narrow bounds.

This probably also explains why labor mobility is so often cited as a factor in maintaining payments equilibrium in interregional relations. It is hard to see how payments disequilibrium could cause labor to move and how this could help restore payments equilibrium;[1] but it is very likely that the mobility of labor between regions should keep wage and cost differences to a minimum and so prevent the emergence in interregional relations of the most intractable cause of payments imbalance.

No less important in keeping interregional cost differentials within narrow limits is the mobility of financial assets. This tends, first of all, to equalize interest rates, the cost of the services of capital; but it is a major factor also in keeping labor-cost differentials from surpassing tolerable limits. We mentioned already that management will be kept from granting and labor from pressing for wage increases if they expect these greatly to lower profits and employment; and that such expectations will arise *i*) if the region has much trade and competition with other regions where costs have not risen and *ii*) if it has no independent employment policy that would stimulate effective demand and so offset the depressing effects on the region's employment and profits of its worsening payments balance with other regions.

[1]See, however, p. 93 and the footnote on that page.

Now an important consequence of the interregional mobility of assets is the impossibility of pursuing independent regional employment policies. One tends to take for granted that economic stabilization is the responsibility of central Government and that regions within a country (and States within the United States) do not engage in independent economic policies. A very potent reason, however, for this state of affairs is the virtual impossibility for a part of an integrated economy to pursue an independent employment and stabilization policy of its own. This has mostly to do with the free movement of assets within a well-integrated economy.

Since financial assets have no transport costs, the integration of their markets leads to the perfect equality of their prices between regions. Where most financial assets are transferable, most asset prices are uniform as between regions; and this precludes independent regional monetary policies. Attempts to stimulate capital formation and spending within a region through a policy of raising asset prices and lowering interest rates in that region would merely lead to an inflow of assets (outflow of capital) and be successful only if it succeeded in lowering interest rates in the rest of the country as well.[2] Similarly, attempts to restrain the economy of a region through a regional policy of raising interest rates and restricting credit would merely lead to an outflow of assets (inflow of capital). As an illustration, consider the impossibility of a regional open-market policy. The open-market buying of securities would leave unaffected asset prices and interest rates, since it would change the quantity of the region's holdings neither of securities nor of money. The securities bought by the region's monetary authority would be immediately replaced by an inflow of securities from other regions; and the money issued would flow out of the region to pay for the inflow of securities. Regional monetary policy therefore can create balance-of-payments deficits or surpluses (outflows or inflows of money); but it cannot influence the region's level of employment and economic activity.

The limits to an independent regional fiscal policy may be not quite as great and are also somewhat different in nature. The smaller and the more open a region, the more restricted the multiplier effects of a change in (local) Government spending on the region's economy and the greater its effects on the region's balance of payments.

[2]It would, however, have a limited effect on the prices of non-transferable assets.

Similarly, Government borrowing within a region, just like open-market policy within a region, affects the payments balance rather than the credit conditions of the region. In short, regional public finance obeys the principles of private finance much more than those of public finance; and it is this fact that limits the scope for fiscal policy. The only exception to this rule is taxation, although the mobility of people and business firms limits regional autonomy and regional divergences also in taxation.

The limitations therefore to a regional fiscal policy are twofold. First of all, its effectiveness is limited, in the sense that the multiplier effects of Government spending on incomes *within the region* are limited. In other words, the cost of a given rise in incomes and employment is high in terms of the extra Government spending needed to create it. Secondly, the cost of achieving a given improvement in economic conditions is high also in terms of the worsening of the balance of payments that a given amount of extra Government spending will bring about.

Let it be stressed, however, that this argument applies, and the limitations pertain, only to regional fiscal policy instituted by and financed within the region itself. A fiscal policy concentrated on a region in order to relieve its localized depression and unemployment but instituted and financed by national Government is an altogether different affair, and usually a much more effective one, mainly because its effect on the region's balance of payments goes in the opposite direction. Extra Government spending within a region, whether out of taxes or borrowing, will improve the region's balance of payments if financed on a nationwide scale but worsen it if financed within the region itself. Our concern here is with the latter case and the limitation it imposes; the former case was cited as one of the reasons for the exceptional smoothness of interregional balance-of-payments adjustment.[3]

B. COST DIFFERENTIALS AS A CONSEQUENCE

Having argued that cost differentials create intractable payments difficulties between nations and are confined within narrow limits among regions, we have yet to discuss them as an equilibrating factor,

[3]See p. 98 above. See also my *Economic Theory and European Economic Integration* (Allen & Unwin, London, 1958) pp. 92–95.

restoring payments equilibrium when disrupted by a primary flow of assets. For the fact is that cost differentials not only exist but can persist indefinitely; and the argument of this section is that they can do so when they serve as an equilibrating factor rather than as a source of payments disequilibrium.

Capital flows or asset movements have mainly been looked upon so far as an equilibrating factor, brought into being to offset a disequilibrium on the current account of the balance of payments. A net flow of assets, however, can also be the primary *cause* of payments imbalance, which calls for or creates an offsetting imbalance between product flows to restore overall balance in external payments. One way to create such imbalance between exports and imports is to change the region's or country's cost and price structure relative to the outside world's.

The simplest reasons for capital flows as the primary cause of imbalance in external payments are regional or national differences in the marginal efficiency of capital. Areas endowed with more or better natural and/or human resources attract an inflow of capital, represented by an outflow of assets, which in equilibrium will be offset (enabling the inflowing capital to be "carried") by an excess inflow of products. Much of the explanation of how this comes about was contained in the last section of the last chapter. The spending on development of the inflowing capital (or even its squandering on high living) will raise activity levels; at the same time, the inflow of money which pays for the outflow of newly created securities will further stimulate activity by easing credit and raising asset values. In the last chapter we stressed the consequent rise in incomes, but price and cost levels will also rise, especially if the situation persists.

This probably explains the coexistence, in many countries, of slow-growing low-cost depressed regions side-by-side with high-cost, fast-growing, prosperous ones. If the presence of conditions especially favorable to the fast growth of the prosperous regions is recognized by the saving public outside as well as inside these regions, they can export assets and import part of the capital needed for their fast growth almost indefinitely. This enables them to enjoy the advantages both of the high volume of spending (consumption and capital formation) that the inflow of capital renders possible, and the favorable terms of trade brought about by the higher-than-elsewhere price, cost and income levels needed to create their import surplus. In other words, an inflow of capital not only supplements the domestically produced output, it also raises real income by creating price changes liable to improve the terms of trade. The relations and contrasts between the North and the South of the United States, between the North of Italy and the Mezzogiorno, and between the Paris and Nord regions and the rest of France, are probably best explained in these terms.

The argument implies that the higher costs and wages of the more prosperous and faster growing regions are a *consequence* of their faster growth, or rather of the inflow of capital engendered by their greater growth potential. The question then naturally arises whether the causal sequence might not also operate the other way around, with the high wages of high-wage regions being the *cause* as well as the consequence of their greater growth potential?[4] This is not the place to enter into a discussion of this topic; but it must be pointed out that as far as the geographical mobility of resources is concerned, high wages repel investment. There is evidence that employers squeezed between the higher costs of their location and the lower prices of competing products produced elsewhere will occasionally try to meet the competition and lower their costs by establishing branches in lower-cost areas. At times whole industries have moved from high- to low-cost regions within the United States; and more recently, some American companies, faced with increased competition from abroad, have lowered their costs by establishing foreign branches in low-cost countries.

In the long run, such migration of industry tends to limit cost differences between regions and nations, because it stimulates investment, general economic activity, and the upward drift of cost and price levels in the low-cost areas. In the short run, however, the capital flow it carries with it worsens the payments situation of the high-cost area. Among regions of the same country, with great interregional mobility of assets, this capital flow may be offset easily enough by an equilibrating flow of other assets. Between different countries, however, such capital flows can be a disruptive force and yet another reason why payments imbalance due to national differences in costs create such hard-to-solve problems.

[4]After all, high wages are supposed to encourage labor-saving innovation as well as labor-saving investment, and both are relevant to growth.

Bibliography to Chapter 10

On the limits that asset mobility imposes on independent monetary and fiscal policies, see R. I. McKinnon and W. E. Oates, "The Implication of International Economic Integration for Monetary, Fiscal and Exchange-Rate Policy," International Finance Section, Dept. of Economics, Princeton U., 1966; R. A. Mundell, "Capital Mobility and Stabilization Policy Under Fixed and Flexible Exchange Rates," *Canadian Journal of Economics and Political Science*, Vol. 29 (1963).

Chapter 11

Sources of imbalance —shifts and disparities in asset demand and supply

A third source of payments imbalance is to be found on the asset account and stems from the many kinds of changes and disparities that can arise either in the demand and structure of demand for holding assets, or in the conditions of their supply. The main common feature, perhaps, of such sources of imbalance is their almost complete neglect in the literature, although their importance is growing with the growth of the international market in assets. In general, an autonomous imbalance on the asset account of the balance of payments has no direct impact on the current account.[1] It affects asset prices and so sets in motion the equilibrating adjustments discussed in chapter 8, leading to equilibrating flows of assets and/or to changes in the net balance of exports and imports. In the last section of the last chapter we discussed the phenomenon of current-account imbalance created to offset and equilibrate a primary imbalance on the capital account; in the following we shall discuss a few more examples of primary imbalance on the capital account.

[1]An exception to this, however, was mentioned at the end of section C of chapter 9.

A. A SHIFT IN PORTFOLIO PREFERENCES

A shift in demand of one area's asset holders away from that area's assets and towards one obtainable only in another area will raise the price of this asset and lower those of others, until enough of it has been transferred to fill this demand and its previous owners are satisfied with the assets received in payment. If the two areas have well-integrated asset markets, such a change in portfolio preferences will involve a minimum of dislocation. There may be some general reshuffling of assets; but the prices of other assets need not change much in order to bring about the equilibrating flow of those assets that will pay the previous owners for surrendering the assets newly favored. The changes in asset prices will be similar in the two areas, reflecting merely the changed portfolio preferences of the two communities jointly; and the main effect of the change in relative asset prices will be the better credit of the issuer of the newly favored asset—and possibly of issuers of similar assets.

When the asset markets of the two areas are not integrated, however, the same change in asset preferences will have a much greater impact on asset prices and probably on the general level of economic activity in the two areas as well. For in this case, the transfer of the newly favored asset can only be paid for in terms of external reserves; and for them to be released in sufficient quantity in the first area and absorbed in the second may require a substantial fall in the former, and rise in the latter, of the prices of other assets.

The effects of these changes in asset prices on spending and investment, and through them on the levels of activity, income, employment, and commodity prices need no further discussion here, except for a reminder that by affecting the flow of commodity trade they diminish the need for the transfer of external reserves. It is also worth noting that such a shift in asset holders' preferences in favor of the second area's assets has all the same effects as a shift in consumers' demand in favor of the second area's products, except for two important differences. First, the shift in asset preferences has no income effects and sets in motion no adjustments of the type discussed in chapter 9. Second, a change in asset preferences, unlike a change in consumers' demand, is a stock adjustment, likely to be completed sooner or later and come to an end.

B. THE FLOW OF CAPITAL FROM DEVELOPED TO DEVELOPING AREAS

Just as differences and changes in portfolio preferences can have an impact on the balance of payments, so may differences in the ratio of the overall demand for holding assets to income. But this is a very long-run factor and its analysis highly tentative. Nevertheless, the overall demand for holding assets and its relation to the total supply of assets has already been mentioned. In chapter 5, the possibility of disequilibrium between the desired asset-to-income ratio and the incremental capital-output ratio was briefly discussed, together with the equilibrating forces that this may create. In chapter 8, we argued that imports and exports of assets, by gradually increasing the gap between the actual and the desired asset-to-income ratio, will in the long run provide inducement for people to harmonize their receipts and expenditures and so bring about equilibrium on the current account of the balance of payments.

It is apparent, however, that the two disequilibria might coincide, mutually offset each other, neutralize and obviate the need for each other's equilibrating forces, and so persist indefinitely. In other words, when a country or region accumulates capital faster (more slowly) than its inhabitants want to add to their accumulated asset holdings, a net flow of assets out of (into) the area can prevent the emergence of the inflationary (deflationary) pressures and of the equilibrating forces generated by these pressures. Indeed, the flow of assets might itself be regarded as an equilibrating force; brought about by, and checking, the inflationary and deflationary pressures.

From the little empirical evidence available on the subject, it seems that technological capital-output ratios in individual industries do not differ greatly nor systematically between developed and underdeveloped economies. On an overall economy-wide basis, however, there are important differences, with the less developed and faster growing areas having significantly higher incremental capital-output ratios in view of their much greater need for new housing, schools, hospitals, shopping centers, public utilities and public services. At the same time, desired asset-to-income ratios are likely to differ the other way around: being higher in developed and lower in developing economies. This was argued at the end of chapter 2. These two differences, and their pulling in opposite directions, render it very likely that the desired asset-to-income ratio should exceed the incremental capital-output ratio in developed economies and fall short of it in developing ones. As was shown in chapter 5, without an international flow of assets, such a discrepancy in the developed economies would make for a secular tendency to unemployment and stagnation; whereas the opposite discrepancy in underdeveloped countries would account for chronic inflationary pressures. Corrective forces will be engendered, of course, and policy can intervene; the main corrective force, probably, being low interest rates in the former and high ones in the latter type of economy.

Whatever the efficacy of specially low or specially high interest rates in influencing and equalizing desired asset-to-income and incremental capital-output ratios within each economy, they can be highly effective in bringing about asset flows and movements of capital. When capital is free to move from developed to developing economies, and does move in response to differences in rates of interest, profitability and pressures in demand, it keeps such differences from becoming too great and proves the simplest and most effective equilibrating force. For what simpler way is there of closing the gap between the desired asset-to-income ratio and the technological capital-output ratio than to export the excess supply of assets or import assets to meet the excess demand? The problem in developed countries is the faster accumulation of productive capacity than of effective demand, and higher potential saving than can be used to provide equipment for the manpower becoming available. The simplest remedy therefore is to export the surplus saving in exchange for foreign assets, thereby slowing the accumulation of productive capacity without slowing the increase in effective demand.[2]

In the developing countries, whose public is unwilling to save and accumulate, and to hold assets in a high-enough ratio to income to provide the capital needed to generate that income, the equally obvious remedy is to import capital and export part of the assets. The inflow of capital supplements insufficient domestic saving and speeds the growth of productive capacity, the outflow of assets slows the rise in effective demand, and both relieve inflationary pressures.[3]

The above reasoning provides as economic rationale for the flow of capital from developed to developing countries. Britain until the First

[2]But an alternative and equally effective remedy is to import the missing manpower. For saving is in surplus in the sense of being more than enough to provide with equipment accretions to the labor force and the labor freed through technical progress. This is why further additions to the labor force through immigration can also eliminate the excess of saving.

[3]Here again, the alternative remedy is to export surplus labor, which will reduce the need for additional productive equipment and raise the economy's propensity to save (since it reduces consumption by no less than it reduces income).

World War and the United States since then have for many decades kept on exporting capital and importing assets without having noticeably raised aggregate spending in relation to aggregate receipts. The reason, presumably, is that the public of these countries wished to accumulate and hold assets in a higher ratio to income than domestic capital accumulation, with its lower capital-output ratio, could generate.[4] This explains why the inflow and accumulation of foreign assets can continue undiminished in developed countries without raising their aggregate spending in relation to aggregate receipts, as was argued in chapter 8.

It is true that imported assets have a yield, which adds to the importing country's income: but the ratio of the market value of the imported assets to their yield is bound to be much higher than the capital-output ratio on domestic investment.

The obverse of all this happens and happened in the underdeveloped countries. Their public presumably is content, and rests content, with accumulating and holding assets that represent only part of their capital stock (the rest being held by foreigners); only slowly, as living standards rise and Westernization proceeds, do social attitudes and institutions change to enhance the desire for accumulating and holding wealth. The rise in a society's desired asset-to-income ratio may perhaps be taken for a sign of its emergence to developed status.

The case discussed in the last chapter of the continued flow of capital within the same country from its slower to faster growing regions might be another example of the same phenomenon. Differences in overall incremental capital-output ratios between slow and fast growing regions are as likely to exist, and for the same reasons, as between developed and developing countries. Contrary differences in desired asset-to-income ratios between different parts of the same country and the same cultural entity are less likely; although even these may exist, owing to the more conservative habits and higher average age of the stabler and less enterprising part of the population that stays behind in the stabler and slower-growing regions.

Let it be stressed again that these are highly speculative surmises, whose further development properly belongs to the theory of growth and whose confirmation or rebuttal must await much more empirical work on the two concepts utilized.

[4]The developed countries of Continental Europe are presently curing the same disease with the alternative remedy, mentioned in the last-but-one footnote: they import foreign labor to man the equipment that their high savings propensities and desired asset-to-income ratios enable them to build.

C. THE UNITED STATES AS THE WORLD'S BANKER

As the third case to be considered in this chapter, we propose to take up a national divergence in the supply, and conditions of supply of secondary assets. We saw in chapter 2 that financial intermediaries make no addition to the net worth of the total stock of assets, because they absorb as many assets as they issue. What they do create is some peculiarity of assets, a convenience, relief from risk, or more often liquidity, which is contained in greater quantity in the assets they issue than in those they absorb; and for which they charge a fee or obtain the difference in earnings between the assets absorbed and those issued.

The financial intermediaries of a nation therefore can be regarded as an industry, which provides the public with services whose usefulness is gauged by the public's willingness to pay for them enough to provide the industry with a living. If a country's financial intermediaries have a comparative advantage over those of other countries, they will, like any other industry, export part of their product and contribute to the country's foreign receipts. Canada's insurance companies, for example, have long been known as important exporters of insurance services and earners of export receipts.

A special problem is created, however, by the export of liquidity. To export liquidity means to provide the outside world with more-liquid assets in exchange for less-liquid ones. Such an exchange increases the outside world's liquidity but also gives the appearance of diminishing the exporting country's; and this might shake the outside world's confidence in the liquidity of the assets it has acquired. Hence the problem, considering that the liquidity of an asset depends on whether people believe in its liquidity and not on whether such belief or the lack of it is justified. Since the United States faces such a problem today, we shall discuss it in more detail.

Ever since the Second World War, foreigners have been accumulating U.S. short-term assets—primarily Treasury bills. Their holdings increased from $6.3 billion in 1948 to their present (1966) value of $26½ billion. At the same time, U.S. residents have accumulated foreign long-term securities, their holdings having increased from $5.1 billion to $21.6 billion over the same period. A little over half of the foreign-held U.S. short-term assets ($14¾ billion) is held by foreign central banks, most of the balance by foreign commercial banks and other foreign financial intermediaries and residents.

Central banks hold U.S. short-term assets as external reserves for the interest they earn and their greater convenience over that of gold —just as the general public holds bank balances for their convenience over that of cash. It is for this reason and in this sense that the U.S. dollar is a key or reserve currency. Other foreign holdings of U.S. short-term assets are explained, partly by some foreign commercial banks' also finding it convenient to hold external currency reserves,[5] partly by the advantages they seem to have for some holders over comparable short-terms assets of their own countries, owing to their greater convenience or higher interest earnings. As to U.S. holdings of foreign long-term assets, they are due, partly to U.S. residents' finding foreign securities more attractive than domestic ones, partly to foreign corporations' finding the U.S. capital market a better one than their own in which to borrow on long term.

The holding of U.S. assets as external reserves by foreign banks shows the world's desire and need for international reserves other than gold; and the choice of the dollar was probably motivated by the importance of the United States in world trade and of New York City as a world financial center. To the extent that foreigners buy U.S. short-term assets because they pay more interest or are otherwise more attractive, and come to the United States here to borrow on long term because it is cheaper, we are exporting liquidity thanks to our comparative advantage in providing it. Foreigners use the American financial system because it, being either more competitive or more efficient than their own, offers them better prices and more value for their money.

Whichever is the reason, we are, as a country, acting as a banker to the rest of the world: borrowing short, lending long, and creating and exporting liquidity in the process. This has raised questions in many people's minds about how long the United States can continue to do so without endangering the foreign-exchange value of the dollar. On one definition of the balance of international payments—the one that used to be the only definition used in official U.S. statistics—an

[5]See p. 80.

inflow of funds in payment for U.S. liquid assets (short-term assets and Government securities regardless of maturity) is considered not a receipt for assets exported but an accomodating transaction and so equivalent to a loss of external reserves. This is why U.S. payments deficits loom so large on the official U.S. definition.

Such a way of looking at the matter has its justification;[6] but it is not very different from, say, regarding the annual $¾ billion export production of South Africa's gold mines as a loss of that country's external reserves. The United States has the same comparative advantage in the production and export of bank liquidity that South Africa has in the production and export of gold. Why then should Americans get nervous over what they consider an excessive export of their liquidity?

The reason lies in the different basis for the use of gold and of bank debt as money. The value and use as money of both depends on confidence: each user's confidence in other users' willingness to accept and use it as money. In the case of gold, however, such confidence was originally based on its value in other uses; and while these have long ago lost their importance, the confidence somehow remained. In the case of bank debt, confidence was established by the promise of convertibility into some other form of money; and as long as the public continues, rightly or wrongly, to consider this crucial, crises of confidence remain a possibility, however sound the bank and prudent its policies.

The dangers of this have long been known and effectively insured against on the national level, because it was recognized that perfect self-protection by the creators of liquidity is impossible and that a stable financial system is essential for the economy. Central-bank money (cash) has everwhere been emancipated from gold by being declared legal tender. Deposit money, too, has been emancipated from cash, in the United States for example by Federal deposit insurance and the willingness (and the public's faith in the willingness) of the Federal Reserve System to act as lender of last resort.

The same problem has not yet been solved in the international sphere. The supply of gold seems insufficient to serve as the only external reserve; and reserve currencies, such as the dollar, suffer

[6]Cf. p. 83.

from the instability inherent in the public's confidence in their moneyness being dependent upon their convertibility into gold. There remains yet to be evolved an international authority, or agreement, or system of insurance, to guarantee the moneyness of whatever instrument of liquidity other than gold is used as external reserve.

Bibliography to Chapter 11

The only subject treated here with a good literature concerns the United States as the world's banker and the U.S. dollar as a reserve currency. See C. P. Kindleberger, "Balance of Payments Deficits and the International Market for Liquidity," International Finance Section, Princeton Univ., 1965; W. S. Salant, "The Balance of Payments of a Financial Center" in W. Fellner *et al., Maintaining and Restoring Balance in International Payments* (Princeton Univ. Press, 1966); P. B. Kenen, "Towards an Atlantic Capital Market," *Lloyds Bank Review,* July 1963; E. Despres, C. P. Kindleberger and W. S. Salant, "The Dollar and World Liquidity—A Minority View," *The Economist,* Feb. 5, 1966.

Chapter 12

Payments balance and economic policy

In much of the second part of this book we were concerned with forces, automatic market forces, that tend to maintain or restore equilibrium in the balance of payments. We argued that the action of these forces is generally smooth and painless in interregional relations but that under the very different conditions of today's international relations, the same forces, though fully capable of preserving international payments equilibrium, would often do so in so painful a way that national authorities prefer most of the time to offset or weaken their action. When their action is offset or weakened, the burden of adjustment is removed or lessened; but so is the tendency towards payments equilibrium. The problem of national policy therefore is twofold . First, how to compromise between the goals of keeping international payments in balance (external equilibrium) and maintaining domestic prosperity and stability (domestic equilibrium) when the two are in conflict; second, how to eliminate the conflict and the need for compromise by developing and pursuing policies or combinations of policies that will simultaneously assure both external and domestic equilibrium. If the second were possible, the first would be unnecessary; but, to judge by events, the second often is not feasible.

Professor Tinbergen has enunciated and proved the formal proposition that n different policy aims can always be achieved simultaneously by using and combining in the right proportions no more than n different policy tools if each affects the n aims differently (in different proportions) than all the other, and all combinations of all the other $(n-1)$ tools. It is not easy to say how many policy aims a national Government has,[1] nor to discern how its different policy tools affect all its many aims. There are, however, two groups of policies, expenditure adjusting and expenditure switching policies, whose effects on the balance of payments and on the domestic economy are so different that it is safe to say that external and domestic equilibrium could always or almost always be achieved together if both groups of policy tools were used. Expenditure switching policies, however, are not used lightly; and when they are not used, external and domestic equilibrium may not always be compatible.

This argument can be illustrated graphically. Measure an economy's aggregate output on the horizontal, its overall balance of external payments on the vertical axis. Domestic equilibrium can then be represented by a vertical straight line, and external equilibrium by a horizontal one. The crossing of the lines gives the point of Bliss, where domestic and external equilibrium are simultaneously attained. The quadrants formed are known as the four zones of Unhappiness and show the combinations of underemployment and payments surplus, overemployment (inflationary pressures) and payments surplus, overemployment and payments deficit, and finally underemployment and payments deficit.

The aim of policy is to get to the point of Bliss from wherever (in whichever zone) one is. Policies can be represented by vectors whose slopes show the relative extent to which they affect the domestic and the external situation, and whose length and direction show the extent to which and the direction in which they are applied. Monetary expansion, for example, can be represented by a vector with a positive slope, pointing North-East. To adopt a combination of policies is to travel along first one then another one of the vectors representing the policies. Figure 2 shows two such combinations.

[1]Domestic equilibrium stands for a number of aims, among them a satisfactory level of employment, degree of price stability and rate of growth. External equilibrium is an exceptionally simple concept; but even this has several definitions (see pp. 80 through 83) and can mean payments equilibrium under different degrees of restraint on trade.

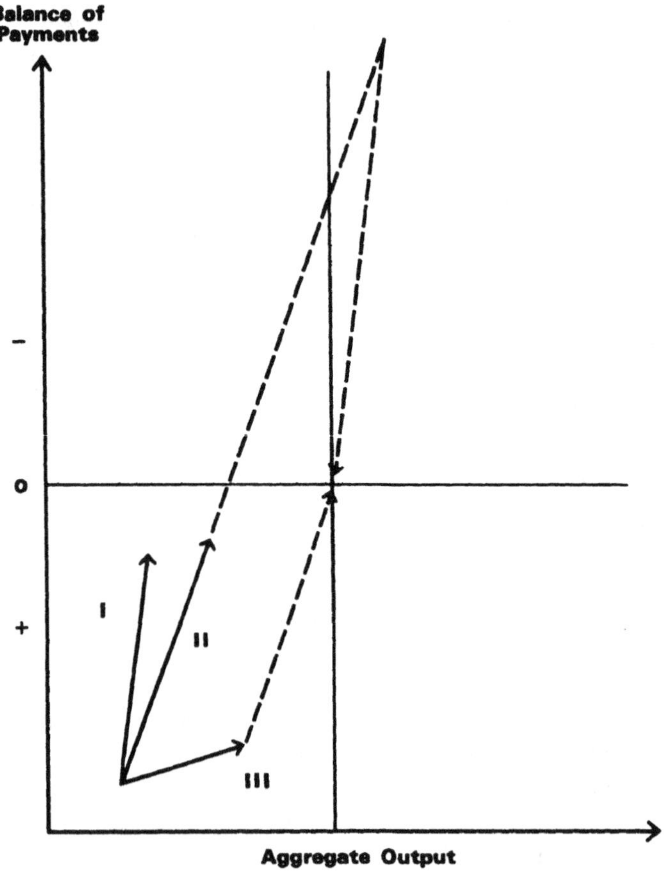

Figure 2

It is obvious that Tinbergen's proposition is true and that one can get to the point of Bliss from anywhere on the diagram with the aid of any two policies represented by vectors with divergent slopes, however small their divergence. But the smaller the difference in slopes, the greater the distance one might have to travel: the more similar the two policies in their effects, the greater the extent to which they might have to be applied in contrary directions and with partially offsetting effects. This is not immaterial, because many policies have undesirable side-effects; and the application of most of them is considered a disturbance. Since the disturbance is the greater, the more intensively policies are applied, there may be limitations to the extent to which similar policies can be applied in contrary directions. In such cases therefore, the length of the path travelled to reach the point of Bliss will not be irrelevant and may be considered an index of the cost of adjustment, which has to be minimized and may become prohibitive. In terms of the diagram, starting out from a disequilibrium situation represented by a point in the South-West zone of Unhappiness, Bliss could be reached at reasonable cost if policies II and III were available; if III were not available, Bliss could still be reached with policies I and II but only at much higher and perhaps prohibitive cost.

In the following, we shall consider expenditure-adjusting policies first, on the provisional assumption that expenditure-switching policies cannot be and are not used. In the next chapter, we shall consider the most important expenditure-switching policy: exchange-rate readjustment.

A. MONETARY AND FISCAL POLICY

Expenditure adjusting policies are those that influence primarily the aggregate level of effective demand. It is convenient to group these into the two categories of monetary and fiscal policy, although monetary policy has several tools; and fiscal policy comprizes, beside the variety of Government spending, a wide range of taxes capable of influencing in various ways both consumer spending and private capital formation. As tools of domestic employment policy, monetary and fiscal policy are usually thought of as two horses pulling in tandem. They also affect the balance of payments in the same direction: expansion worsens and restriction improves it. But while equally expansionist monetary and fiscal policies both worsen the balance of payments and equally restrictive ones improve it, they do so in different ways and to various degrees. A given rise in expenditures, for example, may raise imports by the same amount whether it is due to expansionist fiscal or expansionist monetary policy; but the first will raise interest rates while the second will lower them, so that they will have contrary effects on the movement of funds on the asset account of the balance of payments. This is why in developed countries where the asset account of the balance of payments plays an important role, and where there is scope for domestic policy to influence the inflow and outflow of assets, a judicious choice between or combination of monetary and fiscal policies can go some way toward simultaneously assuring both external and domestic equilibrium.

Also, between countries with large financial centers, the international flow of short-term capital is more important and more immediately responsive to interest-rate differentials than the flow of long-term funds; and this is why a monetary policy known as 'the twist' was developed: an attempt to divorce the movement of short-term rates of interest from that of long-term rates, using the former to create an equilibrating flow of short-term funds between countries, the latter to maintain domestic capital formation and rates of activity and employment at desired levels.

The success of such combinations of fiscal and monetary, or short- and long-term interest rate policies depends on the response of the international flow of capital to changes in interest rates; and this immediately points to several serious limitations. First of all, these combinations of policies are only available to developed and not to developing countries, since only the former can hope, through their own actions, to influence the international flow of assets with a view to dealing with balance-of-payments problems. Secondly, the policy of the twist, as has just been mentioned, has an even more limited scope, since it can be practiced only by a few of the developed countries. Thirdly, international capital flows brought about by changes in interest rates or interest-rate differentials are always the result of stock adjustments and come to an end as soon as these are completed and portfolios have been fully rearranged in response to the new situation. Such adjustment is especially quickly completed when only short-term assets are affected. Even under the most favorable conditions therefore, fiscal and monetary policy combinations or the twist could assure simultaneous external and domestic equilibrium only in the short run. This is enough when the disequilibrium, too, is temporary and the result of a temporary disturbance. When it is not, long-term adjustment is needed; and this is not provided by such combinations of policies.

Lastly, experience with contrary fiscal and monetary policies and with attempts to combine high short- with low long-term interest rates has not so far been very successful. It has been argued, for example, that Britain's attempt in the 1950's to combat her payments difficulties with a high interest-rate policy and to offset the latter's restrictive effects on employment by an expansionary fiscal policy has, indeed, succeeded in maintaining full employment but was the cause of Britain's very slow rate of growth during that period.[2] This would be an example of an undesirable (and in the event unanticipated) side-effect of the kind mentioned on p. 136 above. The U.S. experience, where both these combinations were tried during the past few years, is not very encouraging either.

B. MONETARY POLICY AND THE FORCES OF THE MARKET

Before leaving this topic, it is worth looking at the relation between monetary policy and the equilibrating market forces analyzed in chapter 8. We there argued that the automatic forces of the market could be fully relied upon to maintain balance-of-payments equilibrium if only all members of the economy did their bit in keeping their own individual finances in order. The presence of payments difficulties and the need for deliberate equilibrating policies are, therefore, signs of the central bank's not playing its part or even working counter to the forces of the market. Considering that the central bank is the main agent of monetary policy, this raises the question of what is meant by monetary policy.

The classical gold standard depended upon having every bank, central and commercial, keep a stable ratio between its reserves and liabilities. If these were, indeed, maintained, a $1 million balance-of-payments deficit payable in official reserves would put deflationary pressures on the economy at three levels. Since $1 million in checks drawn on domestic bank accounts would be payable abroad, there would be a $1 million reduction *i*) in the volume of deposit money, *ii*) in the commercial banks' reserves (deposits) with the central bank, and *iii*) in the central bank's own (external) reserves. First of all, therefore, members of the public, trying to replenish their holdings of money, would try to sell assets and so depress asset prices. Secondly, commercial banks, finding their reserve ratios reduced, would be forced to sell assets or restrict credit and so add to the deflationary pressure exerted by the public. Thirdly, the central bank,

[2] Cf. A. Lamfalussy, *The United Kingdom and the Six* (R. Irwin, 1963).

also finding its reserve ratio reduced, would likewise be selling assets or restricting credit; thereby putting additional pressure on the commercial banks further to sell assets and restrict credit.

Today, central banks do not 'play the game', which means that they do not try blindly and mechanically to restore the pre-existing ratio between their holdings of external reserves and the volume of cash outstanding. But what will a central bank do instead? It will usually pursue a monetary policy which in isolation or in combination with other policies is considered appropriate for attaining the policy aims of the moment. For the understanding of such policies, however, it is helpful to establish a few benchmarks to which actual policies can be related.

To begin with, we may regard as our first benchmark the rules of the game under the classical gold standard, as just described. In other words, our first benchmark is the central bank's obeying the rules of the gold-standard game by pursuing an active policy of restricting or expanding the quantity of cash (central bank money) in the hands of commercial banks and the public; so as to make it move in a fixed ratio with variations in its, and the country's, external reserves. This is the policy all central banks, other than the Bank of England, were supposed to follow in the days of the automatic gold standard.

The second benchmark will then be the case where the central bank refrains from doing anything in the face of an outflow or inflow of external reserves, allowing the volume of cash in circulation to change, not in proportion with the stock of external reserves, but by an equal amount. This seems to be the normal behavior of most central banks today, a position of rest, so to speak, when they pursue no particular monetary policy. It is the situation therefore in which changes in a country's external reserves affect the liquidity position of its commercial banking system, thereby exerting expansionary or restrictive pressures on its economy, while its central bank does nothing either to enhance or to relieve these pressures. It is the case we tacitly assumed in chapter 4 when we discussed the creation of outside cash; it would be the behavior of a central bank under gold-standard rules if it were required to maintain 100 per cent reserves; and it actually was the behavior of the Bank of England through most of the 19th century, when she was required by law to maintain 100 per cent reserves on the margin.

The third benchmark is an offsetting policy of the central bank, aimed at relieving and offsetting the pressure of payments deficits and surpluses on the commercial banks but not on the public. Such a policy would accomodate the commercial banks through open-market policies or with a generous rediscount and lending policy in case of a deficit, but mopping up excess liquidity in case of a surplus; all this in a way so as not to offset the effect on asset prices of the public's attempted sale or purchase of securities. In other words, such a policy would allow the quantity of money, M, to change; but only by the amount by which the stock of external reserves is changing.

The fourth and final benchmark is that where the central bank completely sterilizes and offsets the effects on the economy of an outflow or inflow of external reserves. It can do this by maintaining, unchanged, the quantity of money (and of cash) in circulation; that is, by buying assets in the open market at the same rate at which it is losing reserves; or, in the opposite case, by the open-market selling of securities at the rate at which it is gaining reserves. Such a policy offsets the pressure of the public's sale or purchase of assets on asset prices and yields, in addition to sterilizing all pressures on the commercial banks. An important practical example of such a policy is provided by the operations of Britain's Exchange Equalization Account. This agency of the Bank of England is charged with maintaining the par value of the pound sterling by accomodating transactions in the foreign-exchange market. It buys and sells foreign exchange and gold for pounds sterling; and it uses the sterling so obtained, or obtains the sterling so used, in corresponding purchases and sales of treasury bills. In this way, the quantities of cash and money in circulation are kept unchanged in the face of changes in the country's external reserves.

Bibliography to Chapter 12

See, J. Tinbergen, *On the Theory of Economic Policy* (North-Holland, 1952, Amsterdam); H. G. Johnson, "Towards a General Theory of the Balance of Payments," chapter VI in his *International Trade and Economic Growth*, (Allen & Unwin, London, 1958); T. W. Swan, "Longer

Run Problems of the Balance of Payments," in H. W. Arndt & W. M. Corden, eds., *The Australian Economy* (Cheshire, Canberra, Australia, 1963); W. M. Corden, "The Geometric Representation of Policies to Attain Internal and External Balance," *Review of Economic Studies,* Vol. 28 (1960); R. A. Mundell, "The Appropriate Use of Monetary and Fiscal Policy for Internal and External Stability," *I.M.F. Staff Papers,* March 1962; ditto, "The International Disequilibrium System," *Kyklos* Vol. 14 (1961); ditto, "Employment Policy under Flexible Exchange Rates," *Canadian Journal of Economics and Political Science,* Vol. 27 (1961); ditto, "The Monetary Dynamics of International Adjustment under Fixed and Flexible Exchange Rates," *Quarterly Journal of Economics,* Vol. 74 (1960).

Chapter 13

Exchange-rate readjustment

Expenditure switching policies are those that change the direction of home demand between domestic output and imports, and of foreign demand between foreign output and our exports. Since they have a direct impact on the balance of payments, they would seem much simpler and less painful to use for payments adjustment than expenditure adjusting policies, whose effects on external payments are indirect and exerted only through their much stronger effects on the domestic economy. This, indeed, is the customary argument for trade control. All forms of trade control, the restriction of imports, of capital outflows, and the special encouragement of exports, go directly to the root of a payments imbalance and so seem less painful than restrictive fiscal and monetary policy; but they have their own shortcomings and undesirable side-effects. As administrative controls, they fall outside the scope of this book.

The other group of expenditure switching policies are those that change domestic prices relative to foreign ones. The simplest and most effective way of accomplishing this is to change the exchange rate. The alternative way, that of changing the domestic price level or influencing its future course through an incomes or price-and-wage-guidelines policy, seems of limited efficacy and will not be discussed here, since it too is a form of administrative control.

Exchange rates can be changed or allowed to change in a variety of ways. We shall concentrate our discussion on the system presently in force: periodic revisions of exchange rates, kept virtually unchanged between revisions. In discussing the shortcomings of this system, we shall have occasion to deal with a number of alternatives that have been suggested.

A. THE EFFECTS OF EXCHANGE-RATE ADJUSTMENTS

Exchange-rate adjustment is our most potent weapon for correcting payments disequilibrium. It influences behavior not only in the country itself but also in the outside world, affecting exports as well as imports. Since it does not change total demand much but merely deflects demand and resources between the domestic and international sectors, it often needs to be accompanied by fiscal or monetary policy to neutralize its effects on the domestic economy. Devaluation, for example, restricts import demand and stimulates exports; but it also increases domestic demand for import substitutes and restricts potential domestic supply by diverting resources to export production. Devaluation by itself therefore is appropriate only in an economy where a payments deficit coincides with unemployment and excess capacity. In an economy that enjoys domestic equilibrium and needs to have only its payments deficit rectified, restriction of demand (for imports) is inevitable; and this is best achieved by combining devaluation with restrictive fiscal or monetary policy. The latter reduces effective demand, the former confines the reduction in demand to imports. Restrictive policies alone could, if drastic enough, restore payments equilibrium; but only by reducing domestic employment and output as well. Devaluation alone would disrupt domestic equilibrium by creating inflationary pressures and these might even prevent adjustment in the balance of payments.

Indeed, the effects of devaluation on the devaluing country's domestic economy need watching; not only because of our concern over the country's domestic equilibrium, but also because of the repercussions on the balance of payments from changes in aggregate demand.[1] This renders the analysis of the effects of devaluation on the balance of payments rather complex. It is customary, therefore, to deal with it in two stages: analyzing first the impact effect of devaluation on the balance of payments and only afterwards taking into consideration the indirect effects attributable to its influence on incomes and aggregate effective demand. We, too, shall follow this procedure.

Devaluation deflects demand and resources in three ways. In the devaluing country, it raises the prices of internationally traded goods relative to the prices of domestic goods and so deflects demand from imports to import substitutes, from exportables to domestic goods, and may also deflect resources from domestic to international goods. In the outside world, devaluation lowers the prices of internationally traded goods in relation to domestic goods' prices, thus deflecting the outside world's demand and resources in the opposite direction and encouraging the devaluing country's exports. Finally, devaluation often worsens the devaluing country's terms of trade, raising the prices of its imports more than the prices of its exports, thus further encouraging the outflow and discouraging the inflow of goods.

While all these changes in price ratios induce equilibrating changes in the *quantities* of imports and exports, the price changes themselves tend to make matters worse. Exports may increase and imports decline; but worsened terms of trade require more exports in payment for each unit of imports. Similarly, the lower prices foreigners have to pay for our exports may stimulate their purchases; but their greater purchases at lower prices increase our foreign-exchange earnings only if their price elasticity of demand for our exports, η_x, exceeds unity. When this is not the case, devaluation may still improve the payments balance; but only if our price elasticity of demand for imports, η_m, is high enough to make our need for foreign exchange fall more than our foreign-exchange earnings have fallen. Therefore, the effectiveness of devaluation in improving the payments balance depends on these elasticities; it also depends on our price elasticity of supply of exports, ε_x, and the foreigners' price elasticity of supply of our imports, ε_m.

[1]All this may seem, at first, to be in conflict with the statement on the previous page that exchange-rate adjustment "does not change total demand much." But the conflict is only apparent, because there we were concerned with the country's total demand for domestic *and* imported goods; whereas here our concern is with domestic goods only.

To show this dependence formally, it is best to express all values in foreign currency and look at the effect of devaluation on the foreign balance, T_f, defined as the current account of the balance of payments expressed in terms of foreign currency:

$$T_f = X_f - M_f = xp_f - mq_f.$$

All the magnitudes are predevaluation magnitudes, x and m are the physical quantities of exports and imports, p and q are their prices, and the subscript f shows that prices and values are expressed in foreign currency. A change in the foreign balance can then be written as:

$$\Delta T_f = X_f\left(\frac{\Delta x}{x} + \frac{\Delta p_f}{p_f}\right) - M_f\left(\frac{\Delta m}{m} + \frac{\Delta q_f}{q_f}\right)$$

or, in terms of elasticities as:

$$(1) \qquad \Delta T_f = k\left(X_f\,\frac{\varepsilon_x(\eta_x - 1)}{\varepsilon_x + \eta_x(1 + k)} + M_f\,\frac{\eta_m(\varepsilon_m + 1)}{\eta_m + \varepsilon_m(1 + k)}\right),$$

where k is the proportionate increase in the domestic value of the foreign currency.[2]

Expression (1) is a little too complex to discuss; but on the not unrealistic assumption that the supply elasticities, ε_x and ε_m, approach

[2]The last expression can be derived from the previous one by remembering the definition of the four elasticities as:

$$\eta_x = -\frac{\Delta x}{x}\bigg/\frac{\Delta p_f}{p_f}, \qquad \eta_m = -\frac{\Delta m}{m}\bigg/\frac{\Delta q_d}{q_d}, \qquad \varepsilon_x = \frac{\Delta x}{x}\bigg/\frac{\Delta p_d}{p_d}, \qquad \varepsilon_m = \frac{\Delta m}{m}\bigg/\frac{\Delta q_f}{q_f};$$

and by also bearing in mind that the equilibrium relations between prices in foreign and domestic currencies are:

$$p_d = rp_f \qquad \text{and} \qquad q_d = rq_f;$$

and those between proportional price changes are:

$$\frac{\Delta p_d}{p_d} = k + (1 + k)\,\frac{\Delta p_f}{p_f} \qquad \text{and} \qquad \frac{\Delta q_d}{q_d} = k + (1 + k)\,\frac{\Delta q_f}{q_f}.$$

The subscript $_d$ refers to prices and values expressed in domestic currency, r shows the value of a foreign currency unit in terms of domestic currency before devaluation. Its domestic value after devaluation is $\bar{r} = r\ (1 + k)$.

infinity and the devaluation, k, is small, it can be reduced to the much simpler and familiar expression:

$$\Delta T_f = kX_f(\eta_x + \frac{M}{X}\eta_m - 1). \tag{2}$$

Expression (2) will be positive if either the foreigners' elasticity of demand for our exports exceeds unity, or its shortfall from unity is exceeded by our elasticity of demand for imports augmented in the ratio in which imports exceed exports. These, then, are the conditions for devaluation to be successful and improve the balance between foreign-currency availabilities and foreign-currency needs. They are also known as the stability conditions of the foreign-exchange market; and they are very likely to be fulfilled.

However, (1) and (2) show only the impact effect of devaluation on the foreign balance, which would be its only effect if monetary and fiscal policy were to neutralize its influence on levels of income. When this is not the case, the income effects of devaluation on the balance of payments must also be taken into account; and these will usually, though not always, pull in the opposite direction from the impact effect and so tend to offset it.

Devaluation is usually expected to increase effective demand in the devaluing country. When the economy is fully employed, such an increase in demand will merely bid up prices and costs until their rise matches and so nullifies the effects of the initial rise in foreign prices. In such a case therefore, devaluation leads to all-round price increases, with little or no change in the ratio of international to domestic prices and little or no effect on the balance of payments. Hence the need in such cases for restrictive fiscal or monetary policy to accompany devaluation and offset its stimulating effect on domestic incomes.

When the economy of the devaluing country is underemployed, there is scope for a rise in output and real incomes; and devaluation usually brings about such a rise. Increased export production generates additional income and so does the added production of import substitutes if the rise in import prices deflects demand to domestic products. Through their multiplier effects, these increments to income lead to further rises in income and also raise the demand for imports, which will undo some of the impact effect of the devaluation on the foreign balance shown in (1) and (2) above.

The offsetting influence on the balance of payments of such income effects is very similar to the equilibrating influence of income effects discussed in section A of chapter 9 above. There, income effects were shown to offset some of the impact effect of a shift in demand; here, they offset some of the impact effect of currency revaluation. Indeed, one would be tempted to use the same analysis and the same formulae as were used in chapter 9; but here a complication arises that was absent there. There, the shift in demand, ΔZ, showed both its impact effect on the balance of payments and the initial change in each area's incomes, which then, through its multiplier effects, brought about partly offsetting effects on the balance of payments. Here, ΔT_f shows the impact effect of devaluation on the balance of payments; but it represents *only a part* of the initial change in the devaluing country's incomes. It shows, of course, the additional income derived from the additional production of exports and from the additional production of import substitutes if these have been substituted, dollar-for-dollar, for imports rendered too expensive by the devaluation. However, it does not show the increased domestic-currency value, due to devaluation, of the country's imports and exports. These value changes offset each other to the extent that exports pay for imports. But a pre-devaluation excess of imports over exports or of exports over imports is increased in value by devaluation, the latter representing an increase in incomes, the former an increase in absorption and so a diversion of incomes from domestic spending. The added value of such an excess therefore enters into and forms the second part of the initial change in the devaluing country's incomes; as such, it must be added to, or subtracted from, the first part.

It is worth while to express all this in symbols. As already mentioned, the impact effect of devaluation on the balance of payments is ΔT_f, the change in the foreign balance, which shows the initial change in foreign-exchange availabilities. Converting this at the new exchange rate, one can also express it in domestic currency, in terms of which it becomes:

$$r(1 + k)\Delta T_f.$$

The inital effect of devaluation on a country's incomes is best expressed by the change in that country's domestic balance.[3] A country's domestic balance, let us recall, is the difference between its

[3]See, however, the qualification on pp. 150–51 below.

national income and its national expenditure (see p. 77 above); the change in its domestic balance therefore is the change in its national income plus or minus the change in its national expenditure. Now the outside world's domestic balance is nothing else but the devaluing country's foreign balance with its sign reversed. After all, what is foreign currency and the foreign balance for the devaluing country, is domestic currency and the domestic balance from the outside world's point of view.

This far, matters are simple and parallel exactly the analysis of chapter 9 (pp. 106–109). It is also obvious that the initial effect of devaluation on the *devaluing* country's incomes is best expressed by the change in *its* domestic balance; but this, in general, is not the same thing as the domestic-currency value of the change in its foreign balance. The difference between the two becomes clear when one writes down the pre- and the post-devaluation domestic balance of trade in terms of both domestic and foreign currency and then obtains the change by subtracting one from the other:

$$T_d = rT_f, \qquad \overline{T}_d = r(1+k)\overline{T}_f,\text{[4]}$$
$$\overline{T}_d - T_d = r(1+k)\overline{T}_f - rT_f.$$

By adding and subtracting rkT_f, on the right-hand side of the last equation, this can also be written as:

$$\overline{T}_d - T_d = r(1+k)\,(\overline{T}_f - T_f) + rkT_f,$$

or, more simply, as:

$$(1) \qquad \Delta T_d = r(1+k)\,\Delta T_f + kT_d.$$

In words, the change in the domestic balance equals the change in the foreign balance expressed in domestic currency *plus* the change in value of the pre-devaluation domestic balance. These are the two parts of the initial change in incomes discussed in the last-but-two paragraph.

The second part is positive or negative according to whether the pre-devaluation balance of trade is positive or negative. Therefore, the income effect of devaluation on the devaluing country is greater or smaller than an analogy with the argument of chapter 9 would suggest, depending on whether the balance of trade before devalua-

[4]The barred symbols represent post-devaluation values.

tion was favorable or unfavorable. Considering that the income effect of devaluation has an offsetting influence (offsetting the impact effect) on the balance of payments, this is an argument against devaluation in a country, like the United States, that typically combines a large overall payments deficit with an even larger export surplus. On the other hand, in the more common case, where the devaluing country has an import surplus, the offsetting income effect of devaluation will be smaller, and the consequent improvement in the balance of payments greater than might be expected.

It can even happen that the income effect should pull in a perverse direction. If in expression (1) the second part has an opposite sign to that of the first part *and exceeds it* in absolute value, then the domestic balance worsens at the same time that the foreign balance improves, thus creating an income effect that *reinforces*—instead of offsetting—the impact effect of devaluation on the balance of payments. In other words, when devaluation reduces a country's payments deficit as expressed in foreign currency, this reduced deficit can look larger expressed in terms of the country's devalued currency than did the previous larger deficit when converted into domestic currency at the pre-devaluation exchange rate.[5]

All this, the change in the two areas' incomes, in their imports from each other, and the total effect of devaluation on the balance of payments, can be, and needs to be, expressed in symbols. These and their derivation, however, have been relegated to an appendix, in view partly of their complexity, partly of the fact that complex as they are, they are subject to serious qualification.

All the above argument was based on the assumption that the initial change in the effective demand for a country's or area's output is represented by the change in its domestic balance. This seemed the best assumption to make; but it will do only as a first approximation. An improvement in a devaluing country's domestic balance consists of an increase in its export receipts plus a decrease—or minus a lesser

[5]This will happen if imports and exports, and the price elasticities of demand for imports and exports satisfy the following conditions:

$$\frac{M}{X} > \frac{M}{X}\eta_m + \eta_x > 1.$$

For the derivation of this condition and a detailed discussion of the subject, see A. O. Hirschman, "Devaluation and the Trade Balance: A Note," *Review of Economics and Statistics*, Vol. 31 (1949) pp. 50–53.

increase—in its payments for imports. While the former is a change in the effective demand for domestic output, the latter is not. It equals in value such a change; but only if the change in spending on imports is accompanied by a contrary and *equal* change in spending on import substitutes. We assumed this to be so, because it often is a reasonable assumption to make. It is least reasonable and realistic, however, when the change in payments results from a change in prices. For a change in prices may affect the real income represented by an unchanged money income and so prompt people to change their expenditures out of an unchanged money income. If devaluation worsens the devaluing country's terms of trade by raising import prices more than export prices, then it lowers real incomes and is likely to prompt increased expenditures out of given money incomes as a result. In such a case therefore, effective demand for import substitutes is likely to rise by more than spending on imports has fallen.

The same change in the terms of trade is an improvement from the other country's point of view and raises its real income, so causing its people to reduce by more their demand for domestic goods than the increase in their spending on the devaluing country's now cheaper exports. In short, if the terms of trade move against the devaluing country, the income effects of devaluation will be somewhat greater in both countries and have a somewhat greater offsetting influence on the balance of payments than our earlier analysis and the expression derived in the appendix would suggest.[6]

B. THE DIFFICULTIES OF EXCHANGE-RATE READJUSTMENT UNDER THE PRESENT SYSTEM

Exchange-rate readjustment, the best remedy for payments difficulties by the economist's standards, has been little used in practice. Govern-

[6]For the classical first statement of this argument, see Svend Larsen and Lloyd A. Metzler, "Flexible Exchange Rates and the Theory of Employment," *The Review of Economics and Statistics*, Vol. XXXII (1950) pp. 281–99; for a recent review of the entire literature of the subject, see Harry G. Johnson, "The Transfer Problem and Exchange Stability," *Journal of Political Economy*, Vol. 64 (1956) pp. 212–25.

ments are afraid even (or perhaps especially) to mention it. For this, they have several reasons, most of which are aggravated or created by our present system of having virtually fixed exchange rates subject to periodic revision.

One reason is the loss of national prestige that devaluation spells for many people. This has a historical explanation if no logical basis. Because the *spectacular* hyper-inflations of history have been caused by monetary mismanagement, the public blames *all* diminutions in the purchasing power of money on bad policy; and devaluations appear as official admissions of past losses in the purchasing power of money, especially when, as at present, they are widely spaced and attract much publicity.

A second reason is that periodic exchange-rate readjustment (upward as well as downward) encourages speculation in foreign exchange, which greatly aggravates payments difficulties and is further disliked by the monetary authorities, because the speculators' gain is their loss. Exchange-rate readjustment provides capital gains to whoever buys beforehand for resale afterwards a currency that will be appreciated by the revaluation. The system of periodic exchange-rate revision with long periods of exchange stability in-between encourages the speculative seeking of these capital gains very much, because it enables everybody to find out which way exchange rates will be revised if they are revised and so renders this type of speculation virtually riskless.[6] Worse still, by aggravating an already existing balance-of-payments problem, such speculation can precipitate the very action by which the speculators hope to make their gains.

This is why every revaluation must be kept a secret until the moment it happens, and why the authorities must always profess never (or at least never again) to use this means for solving balance-of-payments problems. In other words, exchange-rate readjustment under our present system can force the authorities into the unpleasant position of having to lie about their intentions and impending actions, which is a third reason for their dislike of it.

A fourth reason that militates at least against downward exchange-rate readjustment is the need, under our present system, to overdo rather than underdo devaluation. Since speculation can precipitate

[6]The only 'risk' is the risk of no exchange-rate revision and no capital gains. There is no risk of loss.

devaluation almost by itself, it is essential that no one should even think of the possibility of *further* devaluation at a time when a recent devaluation has just proved the authorities' willingness to take such action. The best way to assure this is to devalue, in the first place, to an excessive rather than to an insufficient extent.[7] Experience has shown this to be a sound principle faithfully followed. This means, however, that under the present system of periodic exchange-rate readjustment, it is much easier for devaluation to change one type of disequilibrium into the opposite type (deficit into surplus) than to restore equilibrium. Also, if exchange-rate revision involves real costs, these will be excessive when the devaluation is excessive.

The real cost of exchange-rate revision is first of all the slight loss of real income implied by the worsening of the terms of trade that devaluation often (though not necessarily) brings about. Another and more important cost is the redistribution of income, with the loss (the burden of adjustment) often imposed on a small segment of the population. Upward revaluation concentrates this loss on exporters, in the form of a loss in their export earnings; devaluation concentrates the loss on those indebted abroad in the form of the increased service (in terms of domestic currency) on debt fixed in foreign currencies.

C. PROPOSALS FOR REFORM

Most economists believe that these costs could be reduced (by reducing the degree of revaluation) and most other objections to exchange-rate revaluation eliminated if some other form of it were adopted. Complete flexibility of exchange rates would, in the opinion of most (though not all) economists, inject too much uncertainty into international economic relations and so discourage it too much; but there are many compromise solutions. One is to allow exchange rates to drift slowly, up to a maximum annual rate of, say, 2 to 3 per cent. Such limited exchange-rate flexibility is believed to be small enough to discourage speculation on foreign-exchange markets[8] and assure

[7]The modern practice, however, of friendly cooperation among central bankers can also do a lot to prevent or obviate the effects of speculation that follows in the wake of a devaluation.

[8]Because much larger gains can be made on many other markets.

enough stability for international trade and foreign lending, yet to provide enough scope for long-run payments adjustments and especially for offsetting differences in the rates at which different countries' cost levels are rising.

Another compromise solution would be to widen the limits within which exchange rates fluctuate around their par values. While this would not resolve the problems created by long-run disparities in the rates at which costs and price levels rise in different countries, it would deal effectively with short-run disturbances and, by making possible losses as well as gains, would curb speculation in foreign exchange. An obvious third alternative would be a combination of these two: wider limits within which exchange rates could fluctuate and a parallel drift of these limits at no more than a maximum annual rate. All these aim at combining limited flexibility with limited stability in some other way than the present system of very narrow fixed limits with their periodic readjustment.[9]

All such compromises would require international agreement and cooperation, because all of them require the monetary authorities to intervene in the foreign-exchange markets; and when exchange rates are flexible or subject to change, different countries' money managers can intervene at cross purposes. The danger of this and the need to prevent it became apparent in the 1930's, when the U.S. dollar, the pound sterling, and the French franc were all devalued, which led to the establishment, first of the Tripartite Monetary Agreement and ultimately of the International Monetary Fund.

One more proposal for reform must be mentioned here, the proposal to establish currency areas comprising several countries. As between different such areas, exchange rates would be freely variable; within each area, exchange rates would be immutably fixed and payments adjustment assured, thanks to much closer economic integration and cooperation, by the same factors that assure the smooth working of interregional payments adjustment.[10]

While these proposed reforms would indeed overcome most or all

[9]Cf. George N. Halm, "The 'Band' Proposal: the Limits of Permissible Exchange Rate Variations," Special Paper in International Economics, International Finance Section, Princeton Univ.

[10]Cf. R. A. Mundell, "The Theory of Optimum Currency Areas," *American Economic Review*, Vol. 51, pp. 657–65, and R. I. McKinnon, "Optimum Currency Areas," *American Economics Review*, Vol. 53, pp. 717–25.

of the earlier mentioned drawbacks of periodic exchange-rate revision, there is an important objection to all of them not hitherto mentioned. Most modern economies have found it impossible to achieve complete price stability simultaneously with the full employment of their labor force and had to accept some compromise between these conflicting aims, sacrificing more or less of the one for the sake of achieving more or less of the other. The cost of each in terms of the other can be represented by what may be called a compromise curve, which resembles and is first cousin to the well-known Phillips curve.[11]

We think of economic policy as bringing a country to a desired point on such a curve, while the position and shape of the curve itself is determined by institutional factors outside the control of conscious policy. One of the institutional factors, however, that affect the position of the curve is the rules, arrangements and attitudes governing exchange-rate revision. While too little is known about this subject, it is likely that the greater the ease of exchange-rate revision or adjustment, the greater the inflationary pressures and the higher the position of the compromise curve. This follows from the asymmetrical rigidity of costs, which creates a ratchet effect, with costs rising when exchange rates rise but not falling when exchange rates fall. If this is so, it is an important argument against flexible exchange rates and easy exchange-rate revision. It is also an important reason for exploring whether the ideal of simultaneous domestic and external equilibrium might not be better pursued, with better hopes of success, through international cooperation.

[11]The Phillips curve shows the rate at which employment can be traded for *wage-rate* stability.

Appendix to Chapter 13

As shown on p. 146 above, the impact effect of devaluation on the balance of trade, expressed in foreign currency, is

$$\Delta T_f = k\left(X_f \frac{\varepsilon_x(\eta_x - 1)}{\varepsilon_x + \eta_x(1+k)} + M_f \frac{\eta_m(\varepsilon_m + 1)}{\eta_m + \varepsilon_m(1+k)} \right).$$

If one assumes

$$\Delta f + \Delta d = 0,$$

that all changes in the propensity to spend abroad are completely offset by contrary changes in the propensity to spend at home, then the initial change in the devaluing country's income is:

$$r(1+k)\Delta T_f + kT_d,$$

and that in the outside world's income is:

$$-\Delta T_f.$$

If, to simplify matters, we choose currency units that render the post-devaluation exchange rate unity:

$$r(1+k) = 1,$$

the total change in the two countries' incomes can be expressed by the system of equations:

$$\begin{aligned} -f_n\Delta Y_n + (1-d_s)\,\Delta Y_s &= -\Delta T_f \\ (1-d_n)\Delta Y_n - \qquad f_s\Delta Y_s &= \Delta T_f + \frac{1-r}{r}T_d \end{aligned}$$

whose solution is:

$$\Delta Y_n = \frac{1-d_s-f_s}{D}\Delta T_f + \frac{1-r}{r}\frac{1-d_s}{D}T_d$$

$$\Delta Y_s = -\frac{1-d_n-f_n}{D}\Delta T_f + \frac{1-r}{r}\frac{f_n}{D}T_d,$$

where the subscripts n and s denote the devaluing country and the outside world respectively, and D is the determinant of the system, its value as shown on p. 108 above. The change in each area's imports from the other is given by the expressions:

$$\Delta F_n = \frac{(1-d_s-f_s)f_n}{D}\Delta T_f + \frac{1-r}{r}\frac{(1-d_s)f_n}{D}T_d$$

$$\Delta F_s = -\frac{(1-d_n-f_n)f_s}{D}\Delta T_f + \frac{1-r}{r}\frac{f_nf_s}{D}T_d;$$

and the total change in the balance of payments therefore is:

$$\Delta B = \Delta T_f - \Delta F_n + \Delta F_s.$$

Substituting terms and rearranging, this becomes:

$$\Delta B = \frac{(1 - g_n)(1 - g_s)}{1 - g_n g_s} \Delta T_f - \frac{1 - r}{r} \frac{(1 - g_s) g_n}{1 - g_n g_s} T_d,$$

where the symbol g has the same meaning as in chapter 9 (p. 107) and represents the response of imports to an initial change in incomes.

Note that the first term on the right-hand side of this expression is identical with expression (1) of chapter 9 (p. 108), which showed the full effect of a shift in demand on the balance of payments. The second term shows the additional effect of devaluation when T_d, the pre-devaluation balance of trade, is not zero. This is negative for an export surplus ($T_d > 0$), positive for an import surplus ($T_d < 0$), thus showing that devaluation will do more good in the latter case than in the former.

Bibliography for Chapter 13

On the subject how to combine exchange-rate adjustment with the proper monetary and fiscal policies to achieve simultaneous external and domestic equilibrium, see the bibliography of the previous chapter.

The effect of exchange-rate readjustment on the balance of payments has a voluminous literature. The most important papers are: J. Robinson, "The Foreign Exchanges" in her *Essays in the Theory of Employment* (Macmillan, London, 1937); Fritz Machlup, "The Theory of Foreign Exchanges," *Economica,* N. S. Vols. 6 & 7 (1939 & 1940) pp. 375–97 & 23–49; both reprinted in *Readings in the Theory of International Trade;* A. O. Hirschman, "Devaluation and the Trade Balance—A Note," *Review of Economic Statistics,* Vol. 31 (1949) pp. 50–53; A. Harberger, "Currency Depreciation, Income and the Balance of Trade," *Journal of Political Economy,* Vol. 58 (195) pp. 47–60; S. S. Alexander, "Effects of a Devaluation on a Trade Balance," *I.M.F. Staff Papers,* 1952, pp. 263–78; ditto, "Effects of a Devaluation: A Simplified Synthesis of Elasticities and Absorption Approaches," *American Economic Review,* Vol. 49 (1959) pp. 22–42; Sho-Chieh Tsiang, "The Role of Money in Trade-Balance Stability: Synthesis of the Elasticity and Absorption Approaches," *American Economic Review,* Vol. 51 (1961) pp. 912–36.

The argument of the chapter follows along the lines of Alexander's second article, except for two differences. One is that while he greatly simplifies his analysis by assuming initial equilibrium in the trade balance,

I considered this too unrealistic to be admissible, even though the analysis of the income effects became much more complex as a result. The other difference is that I tried, in the appendix, to simplify a little the derivation of the expression that shows the total effect of devaluation on the balance of payments.

On the subject of more exchange-rate flexibility, see E. Sohmen, *Flexible Exchange Rates—Theory and Controversy* (University of Chicago Press, Chicago, 1961); G. N. Halm, "The 'Band' Proposal: The Limits of Permissible Exchange Rate Variations," International Finance Section, Princeton University; J. H. Williamson, "The Crawling Peg," International Finance Section, Princeton University; R. A. Mundell, "The Theory of Optimum Currency Areas," *American Economic Review*, Vol. 51 (1961) pp. 657–65; R. I. McKinnon, "Optimum Currency Areas," *American Economic Review*, Vol. 53 (1963) pp. 717–25. For a detailed statement of the argument that greater exchange-rate flexibility would lead to an undesirable shift in the compromise curve, see A. Lanyi's forthcoming paper and doctoral dissertation (Univ. of California, Berkeley).

Chapter 14

The role of international cooperation

We have analyzed at length payments adjustment through the actions of individual decision makers and also dealt with the adjustment policies of the national authorities. Yet to be discussed is the function of international organizations and international cooperation in dealing with the problem of international payments. There are two possible functions for them to perform: to provide external reserves and to impose rules of behavior on national authorities to coordinate their action.

A. THE INTERNATIONAL MONETARY FUND

The I.M.F., established by the Bretton Woods Agreement of 1944, is aimed at doing both. At present, it can provide $25 billion of external reserves in the form of international credit (125 per cent of the $20 billion member-country quotas); although, with each member country required to deposit in gold 25 per cent of its quota, the Fund makes a net contribution of only $20 billion to the world total of international reserves, which is about $100 billion.[1] Even this is only a theoretical upper limit unlikely ever to be reached, since the Fund can only lend as long as its reserves last; and these are likely to become exhausted long before the limits to its lending powers are reached.

The Fund's main regulatory role is the obligation imposed on member countries to keep the values of their currencies within narrow limits of their par values in relation to the U.S. dollar, and to clear with the Fund all contemplated changes in par values. In other words, the present system whereby exchange rates are fixed but occasionally revised is a law of the Fund.

Other regulatory powers of the Fund are its ability to prescribe monetary and fiscal policies to borrowing countries as a condition of lending them external reserves beyond the gold tranche;[2] and its right, never exercised, of declaring 'scarce' the currency of a member so long in payments surplus as to cause the Fund to exhaust its holdings of it.

The Fund has not quite fulfilled the high hopes originally attached to it. The demand for additional reserves has always seemed to exceed the Fund's lending capacity, which had to be supplemented (or displaced), first by U.S. aid, more recently by multilateral credit arrangements among central banks. The Fund's limited role in providing reserves has also limited its authority in enforcing its regulations, since its only sanction is the refusal to lend. But if the Fund has not been able always and fully to enforce its regulations

[1]The other components of this total at the end of 1966 were:

$44 billion monetary gold, including the reserves of the I.M.F.
16 billion official holdings of dollar reserves
7 billion official holdings of pound sterling reserves
18 billion deposit banks' holdings of foreign exchange

$85 billion.

Usually, the deposit banks' holdings of foreign exchange are not included in this total, neither is it customary to add to it the Fund's net contribution, because drawings on the Fund, beyond the withdrawal of the gold tranche originally deposited with it, are not automatic but conditional on the borrower's adopting and pursuing policies approved (and sometimes supervised) by the Fund as conducive to payments adjustment.

[2]More accurately, the Fund makes unconditional loans to a member country not only up to that member's gold tranche (25 per cent of its quota) but beyond that to the further amount that the Fund has lent that member's currency to other member countries.

concerning exchange rates, this was also due to growing scepticism whether a single exchange rate for all of a country's foreign transactions, kept virtually fixed and subject to periodic revision is really the best of all possible arrangements.

The judgement that the additional reserves created by the Fund are and always were inadequate might be thought to be based on some notion of what would constitute an adequate world supply of international reserves. However, it is much easier to argue the need for additional reserves than to ascertain the magnitude of this need; attempts even to define the concept have been unsuccessful so far. It is easy to show that the supply of reserves has grown more slowly than such plausible indicators of the demand as the volume of world trade, or income, or the stock of national moneys; it is hard to make a meaningful statement about the relation of supply and demand now, or in a base period, or at any other time. Yet, it is useful to pose the question even if we cannot answer it.

B. THE ADEQUACY OF RESERVES AND THE BURDEN OF PAYMENT-ADJUSTMENT

In chapter 8, we discussed in detail the role of transferable assets in payments adjustment, the advantages of having a large part of the public's asset holdings transferable, and the difficulties of international payments-adjustment created by the small proportion of assets internationally transferable. All this, however, is not the question at issue here. To create internationally transferable assets, attractive enough for the public to hold and in sufficient volume to assure the automatic adjustment of international payments, would be far too ambitious an undertaking for any international agency at the present time. Our concern here is with the much more modest and quite different problem of what would be an adequate volume of international *reserves.* These are not, like other assets, held by the public as a store of value, because the public does not normally prize international transferability, and for its sake would sacrifice neither the convenience of national moneys nor the yield of other assets.[3] International

[3]Private hoards of gold and foreign accounts in Swiss banks are exceptions, explained largely by people's distrust of the international payments system, or by their efforts to conceal the magnitude of their asset holdings from tax authorities or others.

reserves, designed for accommodating transactions alone, are used and held only by central banks and whoever else engages in accommodating transactions. Reserves would be adequate therefore if they enabled the monetary authorities to resolve balance-of-payments disequilibria. Would any volume of reserves be large enough to do this?

One attempt to answer this question starts from the premise that payments disequilibria are random disturbances, whose probable magnitude and frequency can be estimated and reserves adequate to finance them provided.[4] This is all right as far as it goes; but it does not go far enough. In addition to disturbances that blow over like bad weather and need only patience to endure and reserves to finance, there are also structural imbalances, which are permanent and require adjustment. International cost differentials are an obvious, though by no means only example.

When a payments imbalance is permanent, it calls not only for adjustment but also for temporary financing by the monetary authority until its permanent nature becomes evident, time becomes propitious for adjustment, and the adjustment process takes effect. Moreover, the monetary authority should be, throughout this time, not only in a position to finance the imbalance and close the gap between autonomous external payments and autonomous external receipts, but also under pressure not to postpone adjustment indefinitely but to allow and encourage it as soon as possible. This raises the question how the provision of international reserves affects this pressure.

It is usually taken for granted that the larger a country's reserves the less it will try to remove a payments deficit and prevent the drawing down of its reserves. If this is so, then to augment the volume of international reserves is to postpone adjustment and to increase the demand for reserves *pari passu* with their supply. The Fund's policy of attaching conditions to the granting of credit is designed to prevent or offset this alleged debilitating effect of reserves on the authorities' will to adjust the country's balance of payments. This policy of the Fund, however, has been unpopular with many of its debtors, owing presumably to their recognition of the inequity

[4]Cf. H. R. Heller, "Optimal International Reserves," *Economic Journal*, Vol. 76 (1966), pp. 296–311.

with which the burden of payments-adjustment is distributed among countries and of the Fund's failure so far to remove or to try to remove such inequities.

The one provision in the Fund's charter whereby it could pressure a surplus country into making payments adjustment is the scarce currency provision; and this has never been invoked. By contrast, the conditions the Fund attaches to credits in order to pressure deficit countries into making adjustment are not only a regular feature of its lending policy but one not provided for in the original charter but evolved later and thus clearly representing the Fund's current views.

This points to an important difference between payments adjustment by the deliberate policies of the authorities, and by the automatic forces of the market; that is, through the actions of individual decision makers. Payments adjustment is often painful and burdensome; and since disequilibrium is always a two-way affair, with surpluses as great as deficits, one way to minimize the burden of adjustment is to divide it between the countries in deficit and those in surplus. When adjustment is automatic, the burden is always so divided. The pressure of superfluity may not be quite as great as that of insufficiency; nevertheless, when the pressures stem from disparities between total receipts and total expenditures, and from people's and firms' asset portfolios being too small or too large or containing a disproportionately small or large amount of transferable assets, then there is a fair degree of symmetry between the deficit and the surplus areas in the force of the pressures exerted and in the changes in spending and investment behavior generated.

There is no such symmetry at present in the pressures that dwindling and growing reserves put on central banks holding them. Central banks aim primarily at maintaining employment, stable prices, and conditions favorable to growth in the domestic economy; and they hold reserves so that they may hamstring automatic payments adjustment to the extent necessary to pursue these aims despite payments imbalances and unhindered by the restrictive or expansionary influences that these exert over the economy. The only pressure that reserves exert stems from the fear that they may become exhausted and is directed towards preventing their exhaustion. Monetary authorities must be ever on their guard against the exhaustion of their reserves and temper their domestic stabilization policies with a view to preventing this; but they need take no corresponding precautions to prevent or slow the accumulation of reserves. In contrast therefore to payments adjustment through the automatic forces of the market, payments adjustment through deliberate policy, as we know it today, tends to place all the pressures to adjust and all the burdens of adjustment on the deficit countries. More accurately, policy often aims, in the interests of domestic stability, at preventing automatic payments adjustment, at least for a while, so shifting the need to adjust and the burden of adjustment on to the other country or countries. But when surplus and deficit countries alike engage in such policies, it is always the deficit countries that are forced by the exhaustion of their reserves sooner or later to abandon this policy and to face up to the necessity of making adjustment.

One may ask therefore what reserves or what reserve policies would change this state of affairs and bring about a more equitable division of the burden of payments adjustment between deficit and surplus countries, and then define the adequacy of reserves or reserve policies according to their ability to accomplish this. Unfortunately, it does not seem likely that larger reserves than those now current would be able to remove the present asymmetry by putting pressure on the surplus countries. At least, there is no evidence of any central bank ever having found its external reserves excessive and pursued policies designed to reduce them. By this criterion therefore it seems impossible to answer our question about the adequacy of reserves. No supply of reserves, however great, would put pressure on the surplus countries' monetary authorities to make payments adjustment or allow adjustment to be made.

A more hopeful approach is to ask what rate of reserve creation and what distribution of the newly created reserves would distribute the burden of adjustment more equitably. While the ownership of reserves, however large, puts no pressure on the authorities owning them, the process of accumulating them can and often does. After all, the payments surplus that leads to the accumulation of reserves, and especially a payments surplus on the current account, exerts expansionary pressures on the economy; and when these are inflationary, the authorities will wish or be under pressure to contain and counteract them. Of the many ways of doing this, eliminating the payments surplus is, unfortunately, the least popular; and most of the other anti-inflationary measures tend, if anything, to prolong and enlarge the payments surplus.

There seem to be two asymmetries therefore between deficit and surplus countries as far as the pressures on their authorities are concerned. One is that the pressure on deficit countries to make adjustment increases as their stock of reserves becomes depleted; whereas the pressure on surplus countries grows with the size of their surplus —i.e., not with the stock of reserves but with their rate of accumulation. The second asymmetry is that when deficit countries yield to the pressure of dwindling reserves, they make payments adjustment and thereby also diminish the surpluses of the surplus countries and the pressures resting on them; whereas when surplus countries respond to the inflationary pressures of their surpluses, they will often leave undiminished their surpluses and hence also the deficit countries' deficits and the pressure on them of their dwindling reserves.

The recognition of these asymmetries, coupled with the desirability of an equitable distribution of payments adjustments and their burdens, points the way along which reform of the international monetary system should lie. To begin with, since the main burden of payments adjustment rests on deficit countries with small and dwindling reserves, easing and increasing the availability of reserves to them should be the main aim of reserve creation. Furthermore, since eliminating a deficit imposes a greater burden on developing than on developed countries, they ought to be especially favored when new reserves are created and distributed. For developing countries in deficit have no choice but to restrict the economy, while developed countries usually have many alternatives at their disposal, including policies aimed at changing the magnitude or direction of asset flows. In short, the problem of the adequacy of international reserves has to do not with their volume but with the rate at which to create them, the conditions on which to make them available, and the principles on which to distribute them among various claimants.

While more and easier access to reserves would ease the pressure on the deficit countries; it would be desirable also to encourage payments adjustment by surplus countries. As already mentioned, they often are under inflationary pressure; and a more liberal policy of making additional reserves available to deficit countries would, of course, increase the frequency and severity of inflationary pressures on surplus countries. What is missing is an inducement for them to react to such pressure through payments adjustment rather than through other policies.

The many proposals to render more flexible the present rigid system of exchange rates all share the very important advantage—

not mentioned in chapter 13—that they would render payments adjustment in surplus countries a much more acceptable and attractive anti-inflationary measure. Either widening the limits within which exchange rates can fluctuate, or allowing these limits to drift, or both, would render a small change in exchange rates not only the least painful form of payments adjustment but a highly effective anti-inflationary measure in surplus countries as well. A small upward shift of the exchange rate would directly lower import prices, reduce the upward pressure on the prices of exportables, diminish the rate at which domestic incomes are generated, and slow or arrest the creation of new liquidity and consequent downward pressure on interest rates. No other policy measure attacks the problem in so many ways; and indirect testimony to its effectiveness is the general belief in the expansionary and inflationary effects of its opposite: devaluation. One of the few instances of an upward revision of exchange rates under modern conditions, the 1960 revaluation of the German mark, proved a very successful anti-inflationary measure, much more so than the other measures tried by the German authorities before they decided upon exchange-rate revision.

This combination of liberalizing access to new reserves to ease the pressure on deficit countries and facilitating payments adjustment through exchange-rate revision in order to render it more attractive to surplus countries as an anti-inflationary measure is certainly one, perhaps the most hopeful way in which to diminish the burden of payments-adjustment by dividing it more equally between deficit and surplus countries.

Another way would be the coordination of central banks' monetary policies and agreement among them on when to use which method of adjustment and how best to divide payments adjustment and its burden among the countries affected. An important first step, if only a first step in this direction has already been taken. Within the Fund, and also outside it,[5] there now exists a fair amount of contact among central bankers, which is gradually leading not only to ever-increasing familiarity with each other's problems and means of resolving them

[5]In the Monetary Committee of the European Economic Community, in the Group of Ten (temporarily), in the Bank for International Settlements, in Working Party III of the Organization for Economic Cooperation and Development.

but also to consultation before changes in policy and attempts at coordinating policies, at least with a view to preventing one country's policies imposing additional burdens on others.

The Fund deserves much credit for having brought about this state of affairs; but a lot remains yet to be done. From the very limited and informal coordination of central-bank policies now existing, it is still a long and difficult way to agreement on how to divide the burden of payments-adjustment among all the countries affected and how best to implement such adjustment. The difficulty lies in reaching agreement in particular cases on what would constitute an equitable division of the burden of payments-adjustment. The view adopted in this chapter of considering equitable and desirable a division of the burden of adjustment between deficit and surplus countries admittedly oversimplifies the problem. It is fully acceptable only when the disequilibrium to be corrected has arisen through no fault of any particular country but as a result of the normal ups and downs and random disturbances of economic life. When payments disequilibria can be traced to the faulty or irresponsible economic policies of particular countries, it seems more proper for the country or countries, responsible to bear the main burden of adjustment.

One could probably get fairly general acceptance of this double-barrelled definition of equity, which calls for placing the burden of payments-adjustment on the country whose reprehensible policies created the disequilibrium but would distribute the burden among all countries affected when blame for the disequilibrium cannot clearly be affixed to any one country's policies.

Agreement is much harder, perhaps impossible to achieve when it comes to deciding into which category to place a particular payments disturbance and whether to consider a particular economic policy faulty or inevitable. There are great national differences in economic thinking and political judgement on what constitutes a tolerable degree of unemployment, what is a reasonable rate of price increase, and what an acceptable rate of growth. As long as such differences in judgement persist and are drawn on national lines, it will be hard to reach international agreement on the coordination of national policies, because there will be an international division of opinion both on the nature of particular disturbances and on the feasibility of particular policies in particular countries.

Yet another alternative, to impose a penalty on the accumulation of too large reserves by international agreement and so pressure surplus countries into making payments adjustment, seemed at one stage the most hopeful approach. A proposal to this effect was contained in the original Keynes proposal for an international central bankers' central bank but was rejected.[6] In another and much weakened form (the scarce currency provision), the idea found its way into the charter of the IMF but remained dead letter. Central bankers and the general public alike find it hard to accept the notion that in a debtor-creditor relation, the latter should be deliberately penalized for lending. This is an important reason why easing the burden of deficit countries and making exchange-rate revision easier seem the most hopeful ways of solving the world's payments problems.

Bibliography to Chapter 14

On past international cooperation, see Brian Tew, *International Monetary Cooperation 1946–65*, (Hutchinson Univ. Library, London, 1965). On possible future cooperation, see the many plans for reform; also Fritz Machlup, *Plans for Reform of the International Monetary System*, and Fritz Machlup and Burton G. Malkiel (eds.), *International Monetary Arrangements: The Problem of Choice*, both monographs published by International Finance Section, Department of Economics, Princeton Univ. See also Group of Ten, *Report of the Study Group on the Creation of Reserve Assets*, (U.S. Gov. Printing Office, Washington, 1965); and Working Party No. 3, *The Balance of Payments Adjustment Process* (O.E.C.D., Paris, 1966).

[6]Cf. Joan Robinson, "The International Currency Proposals," *Economic Journal*, Vol. 53 (1943), pp. 161–75.

International liquidity and the reform of the adjustment mechanism*

Payments adjustment and the role of international reserves in facilitating it raise some of the major unsolved economic problems of our day. They can be approached from a number of points of view and at many levels. I propose to stay at the simplest level and discuss the basic aspects of the problem, partly because these are often overlooked in the heat of discussion over the finer points of detail, and partly because the slow administrative procedures of an international and multilingual congress like the present leave me no other choice. I am forced to write this in the midst of the March (1968) gold crisis for delivery half a year later; only by concentrating on the eternal verities of the subject can I hope not to be overtaken by events.

To establish our perspective, let me stress that payments adjustment is the problem; rendering it less painful and less traumatic is the aim. There are many means to this end; increasing the supply and reforming the system of reserves is merely one of them, not necessarily the best but perhaps the one most likely to be adopted.

*Paper given before the Montreal Congress of the International Economic Association, September 1968.

One of the functions of international reserves is to render unnecessary payments-adjustment while seasonal disturbances come full circle and random disturbances offset one another. To an earlier generation of economists this may have seemed the full extent of the story and seasonal and random payments disturbances the only ones to arise.

Reserves, if large enough, can fully resolve this problem; and they obviously ought to. Whether actual reserves are adequate to perform even this limited task we do not know for certain. The only statistical study to date to deal with this question suggests that they are, at least as far as their total supply is concerned.[1]

Unfortunately, there is also another and more intractable type of payments disturbance, which lacks the self-righting quality of seasonal and the mutually offsetting tendency of random disturbances. This is known as chronic or structural payments imbalance.

The term structural imbalance conjures up in one's mind the picture of a wrong pattern of industries—wrong in the sense that it cannot produce exportable output in sufficient quantities to pay for the imports needed to meet the excess of domestic demand over domestic availabilities. In addition to structural imbalance in some such sense, however, there is also another and much more common type of chronic imbalance that has to do not with industrial structure but with international differences in cost levels. These result from differences in the rate at which cost and price levels rise in different countries, which in turn are created by international differences in such things as the bargaining power and militancy of organised labour, or the relative values Government and public opinion attach to full employment and price stability as alternative aims of public policy.

Structural and chronic imbalance are distinguished from random disturbances not so much by their not being random as by creating payments disequilibria of much longer duration. A bad harvest, for example, is a random disturbance; but the development of nylon was a structural disturbance for Japan, whose export markets for silk it closed off probably for good. One must guard, however, against considering every chronic deficit eternal; and it is helpful to recall that

[1]Cf. H. R. Heller, "Optimal International Reserves," *Economic Journal,* Vol. 76 (1966), pp. 296–311.

not so long ago France and not Britain was regarded as the sick man of Europe from a balance-of-payments point of view. In short, the difference between chronic and temporary payments imbalance is a matter of degree: chronic imbalance is one expected to last too long to avoid payments adjustment in response to it. The function of reserves therefore is not only to obviate the need for payments adjustment to seasonal and temporary disturbances but also to facilitate payments adjustment to structural and chronic imbalance. It is this last function or set of functions of reserves that is amiss.

The first of the payments-equilibrating functions of reserves is for their flow from deficit to surplus countries to induce private households, firms and financial institutions to respond to changes in their asset holdings in a way that helps to restore also their respective countries' payments equilibria. This is an important and highly effective function of reserves in maintaining payments equilibrium among the different regions of the same country; in the heyday of the gold standard, it was equally important and effective also in international relations. Today, this function of reserves in international relations is largely extinct, partly because foreign assets are no longer bought and sold in response to small price changes in an age in which exchange control and exchange rate revision are in the realm of practical politics; but mainly because automatic payments adjustment often conflicts with domestic economic policy, and when it does, it is offset and prevented by such policy. Economic policy aimed at domestic policy goals is one of the facts of modern life; and it implies either that automatic payments adjustment is non-operative, having been offset and prevented by such policy, or that its operation is the result of a deliberate policy decision to allow it to operate, this being in conformity with national policy.

This means that in countries that have active economic policies in pursuit of domestic policy goals, the impact of reserves or changes in reserves on payments adjustment must be sought primarily in their influence on the Government's and central bank's policies. This can be classified under three headings. Their first function is to give the authorities in deficit countries time—a breathing space—in which (a) to tell apart chronic imbalance from temporary and random disturbances, (b) to choose the best policies for correcting chronic imbalance even if they take longer to effect, and (c) to wait if necessary for the politically and economically most propitious moment to institute and carry out such policies. The second function of reserves is that their drawing down in deficit countries puts progressively increasing pressure on the authorities to institute and press on with policies designed to remove the deficit. The third function of reserves is that their accumulation in surplus countries exerts pressure on the authorities to institute policies aimed at eliminating the surplus. The first two of these functions are obvious and well known; the third is not at all obvious and hardly known. Yet, the third function is crucial; and this becomes evident when one ignores it for a moment and tries to deduce principles of monetary reform from the first two functions alone, as I believe the Group of Ten and others involved in reforming our reserve system have done.

All seem convinced that payments adjustment, when necessary, must be made by the deficit countries, and that the main problem to resolve is how to give them enough flexibility and breathing space without unduly weakening the pressure they are under to make payments adjustment. On the surface, this seems a reasonable approach. There is bound to be a best policy and a best time for payments adjustment; and more reserves undoubtedly give greater scope for choosing these. They are no help, however, for deciding what is the best; all too often the benefit of hindsight seems indispensable for finding out what would have been the best policy and what the best moment for its adoption. One must also remember that adjustment postponed is hardly ever adjustment avoided; and that postponed adjustment often becomes more painful and more difficult to carry out at a later stage.

These are truths useful to know; but they provide no principle, nor basis on which to build a new system of international reserves. Indeed, it is worth noting that all the better known reform proposals, as well as the reform actually agreed upon at the Rio Conference, sidestep the issue of principle. The upper limit or what is generally quoted in the press as the upper limit to the rate at which Special Drawing Rights are to be issued seems to have been carefully set to keep the world supply of reserves from growing faster than the real volume of world trade, world output, or world transactions is growing. The most therefore that this reform can accomplish is to keep the supply of reserves from declining further in relation to demand. This is much more than nothing, and the reform is desirable also as a symbolic first step towards the use of international paper money. But it cannot and is not meant to eliminate a world shortage of reserves, if there is such a shortage today.

One might argue that there is no such shortage, on the ground that the supply, if not of reserves, at least of reserve credit is highly elastic. For the central bankers of the Group of Ten, apart from holding the deficit countries responsible for payments disequilibria and payments adjustment, are very reasonable men. They appreciate the deficit countries' need for the greater elbow room that more reserves provide, they sympathise with the non-deficit countries' (countries in surplus or equilibrium) double-edged fear of both the inflationary impact on themselves of other countries' continuing deficits and the deflationary impact of the too sudden removal of these deficits; and they have shown great generosity and ingenuity in supplementing existing reserves. The Basle Agreement, multilateral currency swaps, the successive enlargements of IMF quotas and the General Agreement to Borrow have created liquidity at a more lavish rate than the maximum of $10 billion over a five-year period that Special Drawing Rights seem to be scheduled to provide.

If we nevertheless continue to speak of a shortage of reserves, the reason is that all this extra liquidity has brought us no nearer to equilibrium. Payments disequilibria and difficulties have persisted, because, given the tools of adjustment at their disposal, the deficit countries found it too onerous to shoulder the burden of adjustment unaided. Additions to reserve credit, however generous, have postponed but not helped adjustment, because they have shifted none of its burden off the deficit countries' shoulders. In this sense, therefore, the supply of reserves is still short and the system and its operation are still wanting. One might also predict that the Special Drawing Rights will not remedy the situation either if they accomplish no more than to add to reserves on the very modest scale envisaged.

In the days of the automatic gold standard, payments adjustment was relatively smooth and painless, because the flow of gold created as much expansionary pressure in surplus countries as it created deflationary pressure in deficit countries; and the symmetry between these pressures divided the burden of adjustment evenly between the countries losing and those receiving gold, thus minimising the amount of economic dislocation that payments adjustment involved.

This happy state of affairs and the automatic working of the gold standard came to an end in the 1920's when central banks emancipated themselves from mechanical rules of behaviour to become makers of policy, and the Bank of England and the Banque de France set the precedent for neutralising the expansionary effects of the inflow of gold on the domestic economy. Since then, payments difficulties and payments adjustment were associated primarily with deflation, unemployment, restriction of trade, tying of aid, and restraints on the free movement of people and capital—tragic proof that payments adjustment had become more difficult because all its burden weighed only and always on the deficit countries.

The clock cannot be turned back. We cannot and must not return to the automatic gold standard, because we will not and must not unlearn how to stabilise the domestic economy. But the lessons of the gold standard can be learnt and what was good in it adapted to modern conditions. The international flow of reserves used to put deflationary pressures in deficit, expansionary pressures in surplus countries, on private households, business firms and commercial banks. To achieve the same result today, the corresponding pressures must be brought to bear on Governments and central banks in order to make *them* engage in restrictive and expansionary policies. Our international monetary system, as presently constituted, performs the first but not the second half of this task, since the flow of reserves, the IMF, and periodic consultation among central bankers are putting plenty of pressure on deficit but little or none on surplus countries to induce payments adjustment. Yet, the best hope for salvation lies in distributing the burden of payments adjustment between the two sets of countries.

The most direct way of accomplishing this was proposed in the Keynes plan for international monetary co-operation, which suggested the levying of interest not only on reserves borrowed but on reserves owned as well. This would have attached a cost, and so a deterrent, to the holding of reserves directly proportional to their size. Unfortunately, the Bretton Woods Conference lacked the sense and imagination to write such a provision into the charter of the IMF. The idea of paying, instead of receiving interest on funds owned seems to go too much against accepted notions. More acceptable today is the idea of increasing the supply of reserves. The question I propose to investigate is whether this will, or under what conditions it will, put pressure on surplus countries to partake of the task of payments adjustment; for I am convinced that only if it succeeds in doing this will such reform solve our present problems.

In enumerating the functions of reserves in influencing public policy, I mentioned as their least known function, that of pressuring the authorities in surplus countries to institute policies designed to eliminate the surplus. Among the few historical examples are Swedish experience and policy in the immediate postwar period and during the First and Second World War.[2]

Most countries welcome and find useful the accumulation of external reserves, just as individual firms and households find inventories and cash balances useful. Such usefulness, however, is limited; and a payments surplus, if continued long enough, is bound ultimately to cause accumulating reserves to approach or reach saturation point. When this happens, the further accumulation of reserves becomes a symbol and measure of the disadvantages of running a payments surplus and so exerts pressure for its elimination.

The first disadvantage of a balance-of-payments surplus is the use of productive effort and resources for neither consumption, nor capital formation, neither the acquisition of foreign assets, nor the granting of foreign aid, but solely for the accumulation of reserves. When these have become redundant, the expenditure of resources and effort for their further accumulation represents waste. Sweden's embargo on gold imports during the two world wars was the result of their recognising and wishing to avoid such waste. The war-time position of a non-belligerent, able to obtain nothing but gold for its exports, is, of course, a rather special case; and if this is the only example to be found, it merely shows how insufficient the world supply of reserves has been over the past half century.

The second disadvantage of running a payments surplus and accumulating reserves is the concomitant accumulation of liquidity in the hands of the public, the expansionary effects of which often are unwanted and go against the authorities' domestic economic policy. Sweden's postwar policy of putting a levy on exports and raising the par value of the kroner was probably motivated by the desire to eliminate this disadvantage. Unwanted liquidity can, of course, also be mopped up by restrictive monetary policy and without eliminating the export surplus—witness French policy in the 'twenties. But this is not always possible and, when possible, not always desirable even from the country's own point of view.

West German experience at the end of 1959 illustrates the former

[2]The 1960 revaluation of the German mark is an example of the effectiveness of such policies rather than of their motivation.

case. Her attempt to mop up accumulating liquidity through monetary restriction failed, because it also slowed the outflow of long-term capital and created a massive inflow of short-term funds. In other words, whatever effect monetary restriction had in mopping up excess liquidity was offset by its tendency to increase the payments surplus and encourage the inflow of further liquidity. Only the revaluation of the mark in 1960 remedied the situation. Both aspects of Germany's experience, the ineffectiveness of monetary policy as well as the effectiveness of exchange revaluation, seemed novel and surprising at the time; but the increasing international mobility of capital is likely to make them ever more frequent and generally valid. Central bankers have drawn from it the lesson that the scope for independence and national sovereignty in monetary policy is drawing to a close. Another and equally important lesson is that excess liquidity caused by a payments surplus can best be remedied by eliminating the surplus.

I have dealt with these examples at such length, partly because their existence shows that reserves large enough and a payments surplus long-lasting enough can induce surplus countries to make payments adjustment; and partly also because their rarity and exceptional nature show how very inadequate our present supply and system of reserves is for providing such inducement to surplus countries.

As long as a surplus country's reserves are inadequate, the advantages of adding to them outweigh the disadvantages of running a surplus; and if the shortage of reserves is world wide, the deficit countries' restrictive actions are likely to eliminate the surplus country's surplus before its reserves have reached an adequate level. In addition, a world-wide shortage creates a vicious circle; the greater the shortage, the more the burden of adjustment weighs on the deficit countries and increases their need for reserves. As a result, every country wants to accumulate more reserves as added protection against the contingency of running a deficit, and thereby concentrates the burden of adjustment even more exclusively on the deficit countries.

A substantial increase in reserves would very likely be needed to restore to them their lost function of stimulating payments adjustment in surplus countries. We have no past experience to help us ascertain what, in this context, the word substantial means; but neither is it essential to find the exact point of equilibrium, at which the pressures on surplus countries would exactly balance the pressures on deficit countries. We are so far removed from this point at present that coming even a little closer to it would be a great help. The main problem is, not by how much, but in what way to increase reserves in order to prevent their being abused, in the sense of one country's Government diverting resources from other countries.

Many Governments, in South America and elsewhere, pursue a deliberately inflationary policy as a means of taxing their citizens and diverting private resources to public use. The danger to be avoided is an international reserve system that would enable such (and other) Governments to impose an inflationary tax not only on their own citizens but on other countries as well. This is a little tricky, considering that one of the purposes of reserve expansion would be to induce surplus countries to make payments adjustment, partly for fear of inflation or under pressure of inflationary forces. How to achieve the latter, while avoiding the danger of the former, is a problem whose nature will become clearer as we proceed to examine a representative selection of plans for monetary reform.

The one international reserve system actually tried and found successful under modern conditions[3] is the key-currency system. This consists in the use of one country's national currency as external reserves by a group of other countries. If the key-currency country is in chronic imbalance with some of its satellite countries, the latter's loss or gain of reserves puts pressures on them to make payments adjustment through deflationary or expansionary monetary and fiscal policies, through exchange revaluation, or in any other way. The key-currency country cannot readjust its exchange rate in relation to its satellites' currencies but neither is it ever under pressure to do so. (It can, however, be under political pressure to extend reserve credit when the reserves of some of its satellites fall to very low levels.) As long as the key-currency country occupies a middle position among this group of countries as concerns the secular rate of increase of its cost and price level, as long as its economy is large enough compared with theirs, so that fluctuations in the latter's reserves wreak no havoc on its economy, this system works well. For, with the key-currency country's rate of price increase truly average, the number and magni-

[3]By modern conditions, I mean conditions where payments adjustment is a matter of deliberate policy.

tude of unavoidable payments adjustments is minimised and their incidence between surplus and deficit countries well balanced. An important further condition for the satisfactory working of this system is the full freedom of satellite countries to use what means of payments adjustment they deem best from their own point of view. Political pressure brought to bear on them by the key-currency country to revalue or not to revalue their exchanges, or to hold as reserves more of its currency than they wish to, would violate this condition.

The Despres plan is an example of the pure key-currency system.[4] In the gold-exchange standard as we now know it, the key-currency system is combined with a multiple-standard system (gold, dollar, and sterling); and it is not unfair to attribute its problems and crises to the latter's disadvantages out-weighing the former's advantages. An earlier generation of economists has well analysed (in the bimetallism controversy) the problems created by the parallel use of several reserve media; I have nothing to add to their analysis and nothing to say in favour of the system, whose shortcomings have been so dramatically exposed by the secular increase in the proportion of dollar to other reserves.

The Special Drawing Rights agreed upon in Rio might, with luck, give the entire combination of our key-currency and multiple-standard systems a new lease on life if they succeeded in reducing (or at least stabilising) the proportion of dollar to other reserves. The Despres plan would eliminate the multiple standard and its attending problems by demonetizing gold and retaining the dollar as the only reserve medium in a pure key-currency system. The main objection to this is political: the symbolic predominance of the key-currency country over its satellites. This precludes its general adoption, except perhaps parallel with a gold-standard or other key-currency area (e.g., a dollar and a ruble area), with a minimal link or even variable exchange rates between them. The fact that the satellite countries' growing need for

[4]Emile Despres: "Guidelines for International Monetary Reform," Hearings before the Subcommittee on International Exchange and Payments of the Joint Economic Committee, 89th Congress, 1st Session, Part 2 Supplement (1965), pp. 548–561; also, "New Approach to United States Economic Policy," Hearings before the Subcommittee on International Exchange and Payments of the Joint Economic Committee, 89th Congress, 2nd Session, September 9, 1966, pp. 39–42.

external reserves provides the key-currency country with a steady inflow of funds is a lesser objection if the latter can be trusted to re-export these funds by granting aid or lending capital. The United States has a good record in this respect.

Ideally, however, a universal reserve system, where all countries hold the same reserves, is preferable. It would be especially desirable to have a system the communist countries would wish and feel free to join, not only for political reasons but also because they would probably add to the number of those countries willing and anxious to make payments adjustment from a surplus position in order to avoid the waste and misuse of resources a continued payments surplus represents. The functioning of the system would be greatly improved by the participation of more countries with this attitude.

A system of universally acceptable reserves raises the questions: (1) whether these should consist of gold only or of paper certificates held in lieu of or side-by-side with gold, (2) whether the initial supply of such reserves, or their annual rate of growth, or both should be augmented and by how much, and (3) on what terms, what principle, or in exchange for what services, payments or pledges additional reserves should be made available.

One effect of additional reserves is to generate pressures on surplus countries to make payments adjustment; their other effect is to weaken the deficit countries' balance-of-payments discipline by allowing them to run deficits without having to draw down previous accumulations of reserves. (A once-for-all addition to reserves makes possible a temporary deficit; continuous reserve creation allows a limited but permanent deficit.) The relative importance of the two effects depends on the distribution of the new reserves: the larger the share of the deficit countries, the greater the relative importance of the second effect.

Let us consider first the proposal to double the price of gold. Much can be said in favour of a massive initial increase in central bank reserves; and a doubling of their supply need not be unreasonable. Such a shock might well be the most effective way of reducing the value central bankers attach to reserves gained by running a payments surplus and so to make them aware of the latter's disadvantages and willing to act to eliminate a surplus. If this initial increase in external reserves were to leave unchanged the liquidity of private banks, firms and households, its inflationary impact would be minimal, since then, the actions of Governments and central banks alone would be affected. Government action can, of course, also be inflationary; and some countries would be tempted to spend part of their additional reserves promptly. There is evidence to suggest, however, that the majority of developing countries would hold on to additional reserves;[5] and there is little danger of the developed countries' engaging in the inflationary spending of a once-for-all addition to their reserves. At the same time, there would be a general easing of restrictive controls and deflationary policies in deficit countries and correspondingly greater pressures on surplus countries to make adjustment for fear of excessive expansion; but to achieve this is, or ought to be, the very aim of international monetary reform.

These are probable effects of a great initial increase in the value or supply of reserves; they are not likely to be the effects of a doubling of the price of gold. To begin with, any rise in the price of gold would end the use of dollars and sterling as reserve currencies; and their elimination from the world supply of reserves would offset much of the increase in the value of gold reserves. Secondly, doubling the price of gold would almost certainly encourage its speculative hoarding, not right away, of course, but probably within a few years; and this would be likely not only to offset the additional stimulus to gold production but to absorb or more than absorb the entire current output, as it has already done during the past two years. To avoid these undesirable consequences, the price of gold would have to be raised sufficiently to end speculation by convincing speculators that it is overvalued. This might require a three- to four-fold increase in its price. Such an increase, however, would greatly exacerbate and probably render intolerable some of the other disadvantages of a rise in the gold price, not yet mentioned. Private liquidity, in countries where private gold hoards are important, would be very much increased, together with its inflationary effects; and, worst of all, the contrasts and tensions between rich and poor countries would be greatly enhanced. The rich, who hold their reserves in gold, would be enriched; the

[5]Cf. UNCTAD, *International Monetary Issues and the Developing Countries*, Report of the Group of Experts. (United Nations, New York, 1965), paras. 35 and 36.

poor, who hold theirs in reserve currencies or use reserve credit, would not be. South Africa would be enriched, while black Africa would remain poor.

These are serious objections to a raising of the price of gold; but all of them could be avoided, and the advantages retained, by the alternative policy of issuing gold certificates instead. It is immaterial whether these would be additional to gold, like the Special Drawing Rights, or issued, as Professor Triffin suggested, in lieu of gold, by a Gold Conversion Fund against the surrender of each country's reserves. The important thing would be to replace currency reserves and yet to make a substantial addition to the world's total supply of reserves, to make no addition to private liquidity and private inflationary pressures, and to devise and agree upon a more equitable distribution of the newly created reserves than would result from a revaluation of gold. Another important requirement is that the new reserves should be money and not credit. The creation of both weakens the balance-of-payments discipline of deficit countries; but only the creation of money has a chance of imposing balance-of-payments discipline on surplus countries as well.

More problematic than the initial, once-for-all increase in the supply of reserves is the question how and at what rate to keep adding to reserves and catering to the expanding demand for reserves of an expanding world economy. One way would be to create additional reserves at a predetermined rate and distribute them among central banks according to, say, their IMF quotas. This is the method adopted by the Rio Conference. The Special Drawing Rights will create no private liquidity and no private inflationary pressures, they will weaken the balance-of-payments discipline of deficit countries to the extent of their access to additional reserves; but, within such limits as were set in Rio, they would hardly impose on surplus countries a payments discipline additional to what might be imposed by an initial increase in the supply of reserves.

The other way would be to sell additional reserves against real resources to countries in need, creating them only as the demand arose. This is the method of the classical gold standard, where all new reserves had to be bought by the use of resources needed to extract gold. The Stamp Plan and my own would extend the availability of new reserves from countries with underground gold deposits to all those with capacity to produce development goods for development countries.[6] The main rationale of making deficit countries *pay* for new reserves in this way is to provide a safeguard against their financing their deficits by imposing an inflationary tax on surplus countries. It is true that mining gold or manufacturing development goods creates an expansionary effect; but the impact of this falls on the deficit country itself. At a time of full employment in the deficit country, this would be too inflationary to be tolerated, making payments adjustment appear as the less painful alternative; and reserve expansion would not take place. In short, such an arrangement would impose more discipline on deficit countries and confine reserve expansion to periods when they suffered unemployment as well as a loss of reserves.[7]

I should like to close with two comments on the difficulties of reaching agreement on these matters. If the key-currency system cannot be given a new lease on life, it would be better to abolish it and restore to the United States the freedom to alter the exchange rate on the dollar. The French Government are anxious to end the key-currency system; but they are forcing the U.S. Government to defend it, by proposing its abolition not only for the future but retroactively for the past as well. This is what their proposal to raise the price of gold amounts to, since this would force the United States to redeem dollar reserves in gold, thus making her start the new era either with negative reserves or with a repudiation of her moral obligation to foreign holders of dollar reserves. Such an extreme position is obviously unacceptable to the United States.

Let me now come to my second and last point. If I am right that

[6]Cf. Maxwell Stamp, "The Reform of the International Monetary System," *Moorgate & Wall Street*, Summer 1965; and T. Scitovsky, "A New Approach to International Liquidity," *American Economic Review*, Volume 56 (1966), pp. 1212–1220.

[7]A further advantage of both Stamp's and my plan is that resources given up by surplus countries in exchange for their accumulation of reserves would be made available not to deficit countries but to the developing world. Considering that deficit countries are not always the poor, this is an important advantage. General de Gaulle is right in begrudging key-currency countries the resources they get for the paper money they print; but it is unavoidable to give them to someone. The gold standard would subsidise South Africa, Stamp's and my plan the developing countries.

payments adjustment can only be eased by dividing its burden, then reform, to be effective, must generate pressures on surplus countries —but would not central bankers and Governments resist this on principle? Their resistance, probably, is moral rather than political or economic; and it originates in the belief that disequilibrium in economics is an unnatural state of affairs, due to a flaw that can be removed or to someone's fault who must be held responsible for correcting it. Some payments disequilibria undoubtedly can be blamed on some country's reckless or inept policies; and it seems fair enough in such cases to place the entire burden of adjustment on such a country. Many disequilibria, however, are no-one's fault but the consequence of unavoidable differences in the rates at which different countries' cost and price levels rise. One might agree on an example for each type of disequilibrium; but it does not follow that all or even most disequilibria can be so classified. Indeed, it is easy to prove that international agreement on such a classification is impossible.

The main causes for unavoidable payments imbalance are national differences in the amount of unemployment that would assure price stability and national differences in the amount of unemployment considered politically tolerable. One would hope to get international agreement on the unavoidability of a deficit if both its prevention and its removal depended on politically intolerable actions. Such agreement, however, would have the impossible implication of setting different standards for different countries in determining when their economic policies are blameless and when they are at fault. It might imply, for example, that a given economic policy, leading to a given payments deficit in Britain, would be regarded as legitimate and calling for the surplus countries' help to remove the disequilibrium; whereas the identical policy leading to a comparable deficit in, say, Italy, would be regarded as culpable, to be removed by Italy's own efforts alone. Surely, we have not yet reached the level of enlightenment and international understanding necessary for such an attitude; if not, it is equally hopeless—except in very special cases—to reach international agreement on which disequilibria should be tackled by concerted action and which ones left to be eliminated by the country or countries supposed to have caused them.

What is the solution of the dilemma? The best solution to my mind is to consider all disequilibria the joint responsibility of all countries affected; accepting minor abuse as a small price to pay for a workable system, and guarding against major abuse by the proper control of reserve creation.

Unfortunately, our money managers seem to lean in the opposite direction. They would like to affix guilt for chronic payments imbalance whenever possible; and when this predilection is combined with a value judgement that places price stability on a higher pedestal than full employment, it is hard to resist condemning almost every chronic imbalance in deficit (though never in surplus) countries. Deep down they must often feel doubt—to judge by their great lenience in lightening or suspending sentence on those found guilty. A true solution, however, of our monetary problems must await a reformed attitude and an international division, not only of labour and its benefits, but of the adjustment burden as well.

INDEX*

***Relates only to chapters 1 through 14. Not indexed are concepts listed in the Table of Contents and those that, like cash, interest, liquidity, recur too often for their full indexing to be useful. The definitions of the latter, however, are indexed, printed in italics.**

For Product Safety Concerns and Information please contact our EU representative GPSR@taylorandfrancis.com
Taylor & Francis Verlag GmbH, Kaufingerstraße 24, 80331 München, Germany

www.ingramcontent.com/pod-product-compliance
Lightning Source LLC
LaVergne TN
LVHW011132300926
849160LV00008B/611
* 9 7 8 1 1 3 8 2 1 7 9 7 3 *